Jesus, the Word, and the Way of the Cross

An Engagement with Muslims, Buddhists, and Other Peoples of Faith

Mark W. Thomsen

Lutheran University Press
Minneapolis, Minnesota

Jesus, the Word, and the Way of the Cross
An Engagement with Muslims, Buddhists, and Other Peoples of Faith
Mark W. Thomsen

Publication of this book is funded in part by a grant from ELCA Global Mission.

Cover: The forty-four foot "Tower of the Four Winds" is located on a high hill in Blair, Nebraska, overlooking Dana College and the Missouri River Valley. The tower and mosaic designed by F.W. Thomsen (the author's uncle) were inspired by the visions of an Oglala Sioux "holy man," Black Elk (1863-1950) as described by the poet John G. Neihardt in *Black Elk Speaks* (1932).

Symbols from visions of Black Elk appear in the mosaic. The vertical arm represents the Road of Life, and the horizontal arm represents the Road of Suffering. In Sioux mythology where these roads cross is a holy place. A giant cottonwood tree, at that crossing point—the center of the world, shelters all the children of the Great Spirit's creation. At the center of series of hoops symbolizing a unified human community is a human figure. Black Elk saw this "Messianic Person" against the tree of life, a figure that was neither Native American nor White, transcending the enmity that threatened the Sioux people.

Thomsen has juxtaposed these images in a way that immediately appears to be the crucified Christ.

Photo by Dr. Charles Bagby, Blair, Nebraska.

Library of Congress Cataloging-in-Publication Data
Thomsen, Mark W., 1931-
 Jesus, the Word, and the way of the Cross : an engagement with Muslims, Buddhists, other peoples of faith / Mark W. Thomsen. – [Rev. ed.].
    p. cm.
 Rev. ed. of: The Word and the way of the Cross. c1993.
 Includes bibliographical references.
 ISBN-13: 978-1-932688-34-4 (alk. paper)
 ISBN-10: 1-932688-34-X (alk. paper)
 1. Missions to Buddhists. 2. Missions to Muslims. 3. Jesus Christ–Crucifixion. I. Thomsen, Mark W., 1931- Word and the way of the Cross. II. Title.
 BV2618.T48 2008
 266.008'82943–dc22
                          2007047771

Lutheran University Press • PO Box 390759 • Minneapolis, MN 55439
Manufactured in the United States of America

Table of Contents

Foreword

How do we engage the other? This is a defining question for mission today. I did not reach this conclusion by carefully reflecting on the topic but by stumbling upon it as I went about my daily routine.

I was returning to Chicago from a meeting of the National Council of Churches of Christ in the USA. This particular day I decided to take public transportation rather than asking a classmate from seminary for a ride as I usually do. After some initial research I knew that I could pick up the M-60 bus in front of Columbia University to La Guardia airport. At the bus stop a homeless woman stood by me and engaged me in conversation. Through her questioning she knew I was a pastor, who had attended a meeting in New York, on his way home to Chicago, taking public transportation for the first time and anxious about either getting lost or missing the stop. I could feel my apprehensions bubbling up inside, apprehensions about the whole enterprise and about this stranger.

The woman told me that she would help me, and proceeded to place some coins in the saxophone case of a man that was playing nearby, "Play some good music for my friend, he is from Chicago." As we entered the bus, the woman sat behind me. The bus began its journey and turned right onto 125th Street and while traversing through Harlem the woman gave me a tour of this famous street, pointing to landmarks and places of importance in the civil rights movement and to race relations in the City of New York. I listened to the woman, but my fears, apprehensions, and yes, my judgmental and stereotypical attitude precluded me from engaging her. I immersed myself in reading a newspaper. That's when I stumbled upon the question of how to engage the other, and turning back to talk to the woman I noticed she was gone. The bus came to a stop and when the driver shouted, "Sir, this is your stop," no one responded. The driver turned back and said "Father, this is your stop." Being the only one dressed like a "father" (I was wearing a black clerical shirt and a black suit) I went to the front of the bus to exit, and out of curiosity asked the driver, "How did you know this was my stop?" He responded, "Your friend told me you were going to the airport and asked me to make sure you did not miss your stop."

At that time theological questions became spears piercing the heart, texts from Scripture flowed through my mind shaming me as I ignored the "other" because she was a homeless person, a "bag lady' from the streets of New York City.

A quick look at the world situation today may lead us to conclude that many of our problems and challenges emerge as a result of how we engage the other, whoever that other is, whether cultural, racial, political, sexual, or religious; e.g. the genocide in Rwanda, blue and red States, straight and gay, Israelis and Palestinians, September 11 and the War on Terror.

How we see and understand the other will determine the ways in which we will engage him or her. That engagement has the possibility of being a path toward dialogue and conversation, leading to deeper understanding, opening opportunities for building relationships of trust, and cementing the way for a peaceful coexistence.

Building upon years of missionary service and academic research, Dr. Mark Thomsen engages this defining question for mission of the "other" in the 21st century as an increasingly religious one. Without compromising the Christian witness, he presents a way for engaging in intimate dialogue with the religious other, a dialogue that is respectful and truthful, while yet addressing old forms and paradigms that diminish the religious "other" and the God in whose name he or she is engaged.

God in the Crucified Jesus became ultimately significant for all time, in all places, and for all peoples. It is the Cross of Christ that points to the "costly suffering love incarnate in the cosmic crucified." That Cross is an invitation to humbleness, self-giving, and vulnerability "…in contrast to all forms of Christian arrogance, intolerance, and imperialism." This arrogance, intolerance, and imperialistic behavior are not particular to Christianity only. As I write these words, the British news magazine *The Economist*, has just published a special report on religion under the heading "*The New Wars of Religion.*" The report points toward the growing number of conflicts with an increasing religious dimension. Quoting Philip

Jenkins the report claims " ... that when historians look back at this century, they will probably see religion as 'the prime animating and destructive force in human affairs, guiding attitudes to political liberties and obligation, concepts of nationhood and, of course, conflicts and wars.'" Sobering words indeed. However, this cosmic crucified in whom we encounter "God's costly love," re-dimensions our perspective of the other, enabling us to see in him or her "the face of God" (Gen 33: 10b), thus overcoming attitudes and behaviors that do become "destructive forces" among all of God's children. Nothing is more poignant to this reality than the Cross of Christ, "God's 'Yes' to the World" as Douglas John Hall has described it. Only from this vantage point of Jesus' vulnerability, can we truly engage the other in mission: "It is essential that we proclaim a Gospel shaped by Jesus Crucified rather than a message shaped by our cultural values and norms. It is essential that it is Jesus Crucified, not ourselves, who defines God and the mission of God." That mission is to restore community with all of God's people, for "all this is from God, who reconciled us to himself through Christ and has given us the ministry of reconciliation" (2 Cor 5:18).

Dr. Thomsen's personal testimony is an invitation to "*al seguimiento a Jesús,*" to follow Jesus and to participate in God's saving mission: "I can understand why people in a world of suffering are agnostics or atheists; however, I cannot understand why people who believe in Jesus Christ do not want to speak about the Gospel, share it, preach it, in order that others might trust in it."

Throughout these pages the reader will find a thorough and critical exposition of the Christ event and the work of Christ and its significance for humanity. The theological insights offered here are of great value for Christian witness and mission in an increasingly religious pluralistic world.

Dr. Thomsen creatively achieves the aim stated at the outset of his book: "That a focus upon the creative, transforming, costly, suffering love of God concretely identified in Jesus is the most authentic way to articulate the Gospel among Muslim and Buddhist communities today."

> The Rev. Rafael Malpica Padilla
> Executive Director, ELCA Global Mission
> Christ the King, 2007

Reference: The Economist *In God's Name: a Special Report on Religion and Public Life,* November 3, 2007 (The Economist Newspaper Limited: New York, NY) page 4.

Introduction

According to recent statistics the global human family numbers 6.2 billion people including: 2.2 billion Christians, 1.1 billion Muslims, and 350 million Buddhists.[1] Christians engaged with Muslims and Buddhists are involved in a privileged and challenging opportunity. Islam and Buddhism have had the capacity to transcend cultural and religious boundaries, permeating with human and divine values the lives of people and nations. They also offer wisdom and insight to Christian people and they challenge the Christian faith in unique ways.

Islam challenges the assertion that the Word of God came to expression not only in the words of a Holy Book, but in the life and humanity of Jesus. Islam also questions the reality of Jesus, as the Messiah, being executed on a Roman cross. Theravada and Zen Buddhism's challenge goes even deeper when they do not assert the reality of God or the relevance of God for human salvation or transformation. Of even greater significance for all religious communities is the challenge to be reconciling and peace making peoples. In a world which is explosively divided, alienation, estrangement, conflict and violence permeate our common human family. Often our religious communities contribute to the violence rather than participate in healing and reconciliation. We are all challenged to quests for mutual understanding and we are all called to common searches for justice, reconciliation and peace.

Christians are compelled among Buddhist and Muslim peoples to seek to live and think through their faith and lives with integrity. On the one hand, what is it that Christians share with Muslims and Buddhists that binds them as one with the human family? On the other, what are the marks of our particular vision which we believe are so significant that we wish to share them with the interfaith community? If the answer is wrapped up in Jesus, how do we articulate our witness to the "Good News" we believe we have found?

Christians know that their lives and cultures have often detracted from rather than enhanced their witness. How then do we approach Muslims and Buddhists in order that our witness through words and actions may not detract from our witness but authentically witness to Jesus as servant of God and Prince of Peace?

In exploring Christian engagement with Muslims, Buddhists and other peoples of faith, the discussion will focus upon the centrality of Jesus. A focus upon Jesus as portrayed in the New Testament is essential to our discussion because Jesus is recognized as a person of great significance within the Muslim community and also of interest within the Buddhist community. Within Islam, Jesus is designated not only as one of the prophets sent to the children of Israel, but as a word from God (Surah 3:45); a sign and a mercy from God (Surah 19:21); one strengthened with the Holy Spirit (Surah 2:253); a witness on the day of judgment (Surah 4:159); and like Adam God created him by direct command in Mary's womb (Surah 3:47). The Qur'an invites the Muslim community to be fascinated by Jesus. Buddhism, unlike Islam, predates Christianity by about 500 years. There seems to have been little contact between Buddhists and Christians until about two hundred years ago.[2] Today, however, Jesus is often recognized by many Buddhists as a person of deep spiritual insight. Jesus' non-violent lifestyle is particularly attractive to Buddhist peoples who have traditionally with the Buddha been committed to non-violence. The Christian does not have to create an interest in Jesus; it is already present.

The focus of this statement will be upon Jesus, but particularly upon Jesus crucified. It is Jesus crucified who is designated Lord by early Christians. The early apostles proclaimed that the one with nail-pierced hands was raised from the dead, sits at the right hand of God as cosmic Lord and Savior. The kingdom/reign of God had come near and was present in the prophet of the kingdom who had been put to death in Jerusalem. God had been seen, heard and touched in the Prince of Peace who chose not to inflict violence in the struggle of the Kingdom of God. The resurrection proclaimed that the future belonged to this tortured figure through whom God brings life from death. The depth and breadth of the significance of Jesus' non-violent prophetic ministry and the violent death inflicted upon him is often lost in a simplistic theory of the atonement.

It is the thesis of this document that a focus upon the creative, transforming, costly, suffering love of God concretely identified in Jesus is the most authentic way to articulate the gospel among Muslim and Buddhist communities today. A Christian witness pointing to Jesus crucified addresses a number of specific and significant issues that relate directly to engagement with these religious communities.

First, within the world of Islam and Buddhism, Jesus and the cross of Jesus speak powerfully of God who calls Christians as disciples to take up their own crosses and follow Jesus crucified. Christians as disciples are called to proclaim the gospel of this self-giving, vulnerable One. That is the *Word of Jesus and Jesus' Cross*. However, they are also called to follow this Jesus into the pain of human existence; to participate in the humble, self-giving vulnerable love of the mission of this Jesus who incarnates the coming of God's kingdom. That is the *Way of the Cross*. In contrast to all forms of Christian arrogance, intolerance and imperialism, Jesus' disciples are called to be servants washing people's feet, "Christ-minded" persons molded by the Cosmic Crucified: "Let the same mind be in you that was in Christ Jesus . . ." (Phil 2:5-11).

Second, in relationship to Islam, a focus on Jesus' non-violent mission and crucifixion emphasizes that God and the coming of the reign of God is marked by vulnerability. Jesus' vulnerable mission ending in a violent death is distinct from Muhammad who faced persecution and then successfully defended the small community of believers to the point where he reentered the city of Mecca. Muhammad's role as prophetic guide to unite people from tribal conflict and warfare molded the Muslim vision of spirituality and communal justice. It also inspired a theology which tended to emphasize the invulnerability of God. The mission of Jesus crucified tended to mold a Christian vision (soon lost in a militant Christendom) of a vulnerable God and a non-violent coming of the reign of God.

Third, within the Theravada Buddhist context, Jesus as the Cosmic Crucified speaks powerfully and effectively of divine costly love–the willingness of God to share suffering and brokenness (suffering or "unsatisfactoriness" is a basic Buddhist motif) in order to transform life marked by suffering and brokenness. Buddhists who live without trust in God as the source of the transformation of life may find interesting this new and different vision.

Fourth, a Jesus movement will be called into a radical participation in the quest for justice, reconciliation and peace. One-sixth of the world's population lives on less than $1.00 a day. This means that 800 million live with diets that do not allow for the full development of their bodies or minds. Thirty thousand children die everyday of malnutrition or treatable diseases. Thirteen million orphans live on the continent of Africa because their parents have died of AIDS. Jesus as Servant of God calls disciples into a quest for healing and justice. Furthermore, Jesus as Prince of Peace in the midst of a violent world calls for a non-violent mission for peace on the earth. The one who rejected violence but who willingly bore violence calls for a radical but sensitive ministry marked by compassion and quests for righteousness and peace. They are called to be "militant pacifists" or non-violent resisters for the sake of the Kingdom/Reign of God.

Finally, it will be noted that the significance of Jesus crucified and risen for all times and places is not that one must meet and receive Jesus in order to be saved. Rather, that the creative, transforming suffering love of God concretized in Jesus is the transforming power within and of all creation. That creative love is not bound or limited within a historical Jesus or Christian box but is active in every people and culture; however, Jesus calls the Jesus people to participate in God's transforming and saving work.

In a multiplicity of ways the New Testament faith claims that Jesus crucified and risen has transforming significance for the whole world and the totality of creation. I have used the phrase "Cosmic Crucified" to designate this affirmation of faith. The question is how is Jesus significant for the totality of creation? This is an essential question in our inter-faith journey.

This book is written for Christians who are world citizens and who recognize that they make up a minority of the world's six billion plus inhabitants. It is hoped that this vision of Jesus and Jesus' cross will enable us to recognize the radical nature of our faith and the call of Jesus to participate in a community that will actually be observed as foolishness and out of step with contemporary values and institutionalized faiths. Particularly, it is hoped that a striking contrast will be seen between Jesus and contemporary behavioral expressions of American Christianity. If this is possible we also may actually be able to share Jesus with the world.

Chapter 1

Jesus and the Cross: The Presence of the Kingdom of God

Jesus and the Kingdom/Reign of God

In focusing on both Jesus and the cross it is necessary to place Jesus' death within Jesus' message and mission. That message and mission was focused upon God and the Reign (Kingdom) of God. The cross of Jesus meant dying to private dreams in order to participate in the vision of the kingdom of God. A theology of the cross is grounded in the prayer of Jesus that led to his cross: "Not my will but your will be done." The Gospels witness to the reality that Jesus' mission and death were not the private dream of a Jewish carpenter but were rooted in the vision of the Reality whom Jesus addressed as "Father." If nothing else, Jesus was a person possessed by the reality of God. Jesus believed he was called by God, empowered by the Spirit of God, led by God, even if it meant being faithful to a vision that ultimately led to the horror of Golgatha. Jesus witnessed to God, spoke of God—the central theme of his proclamation was the kingdom of God—and his most powerful gift was a baptism into the Spirit of God. From the perspective of Jesus and the early disciples, Jesus surrendered his heart, mind, will and life to God. The cross signified dying to personal dreams and visions in order to be open to the reign of God.

We are apt to forget as Christians the Markan account of the rich young man who came to Jesus asking about the path to eternal life (Mk 10:17ff). The young man said, "Good teacher, what must I do to inherit eternal life." Jesus replied, "Why do you call me good? **No one is good but God alone.** "Christians in dialogue with Muslims, Buddhists and peoples of other faiths must build on this foundation upon which Jesus trusted. "No one is good but the one God." All humanity and the totality of reality are created, affirmed and continually transformed by the one God, by God alone. Jesus' vision of God and the Reign of God are identified by a number of remarkable characteristics.

God is Abba (Father)

For many, God is a terrifying presence, a cosmic tyrant, the heavenly law enforcer, the capricious cosmic power demanding obedience or sacrificial bribes for survival in the divine presence. For others, God is an unknown unfathomable mystery or an illusion created by immature minds terrified at being alone in a dark eternal night.

In contrast, Jesus leads his followers into the inner family circle of a father/a mother, and his/her children. The cosmic Abba is like an anxious parent waiting for a wayward son or daughter to return after a self-destructive adventure into promiscuous sex and destructive addictions (Lk 15). The Abba is like a seeking shepherd risking danger, injury and death in order to find a lost lamb in the Judean wilderness (Lk 15). The Abba is like a wealthy entrepreneur willing to pay a days' wages to laborers who bore the burden of the midday Arizona heat as well as to the one who showed up late and sweat for only an hour (Mt 20:1-15). The Abba is like the physician whose vocation is to heal the sick (Mt 9:9-13). The vision of Jesus allows people to see life as dwelling in a garden marked by grace, by green pastures, hillsides filled with lilies and transected by brooks of sparkling, life-giving water. This is a garden whose overseer desires children to find life and hope within a hope-filled Reign of God. This is a contrast between waterless desert and nourishing meadows, between visions of hell and nothingness and the presence of grace.

The Abba is Awesome Wonder

The intimacy of personal relationships with the cosmic Abba however, is not a trivial relationship with a cosmic genie at the beck and call of the human partner. Walking in relationship with the Abba of the universe is a relationship marked by awesome wonder. Jesus teaches his disciples to pray, saying, "Father, Let your name be holy; Your kingdom come" (Lk 11:2). "Holy" marks the distinction between that which is God and that which is not God. In Isaiah's vision (Is 6:1-6) the prophet is overwhelmed by that which causes temple foundations to shake and that which creates in the prophet an awareness of spiritual brokenness, necessitating forgiveness and purification flowing from God's generous presence. The Cosmic Abba is the awesome wonder, holding galaxies in the divine embrace and graciously pouring out life-creating and affirming love upon the whole of cosmic reality. Both intimacy and awesome wonder are a reality in relationship with the Universal Abba (Ps 8, Is 40).

The Cosmic Abba Nurtures and Sustains Life

The teachings of Jesus are filled with images of the Abba who nurtures all of life. It is God, the Cosmic Abba, who clothes the lilies that transform the Galilean countryside into images of royal beauty (Mt 6:27); it is God who feeds the birds of the air (Mt 6:26) and knows when even a sparrow falls in death (Mt 10:29). It is the Cosmic Abba who numbers the hairs of the human head and knows the count of their decreasing presence as agedness devours youth (Mt 10:30). It is God who brings forth life upon the planet earth as the perfect Father makes possible the life-creating energy of sunshine and rain (Mt 5:43-48).

The Abba of the Universe Delights in Humanity

The Biblical story places humanity at the center of the cosmic web of life. The creation narrative of Genesis climaxes with the human couple who are created in the image of God. They have the potential for relationships with God, others and themselves and the created order. They have potential for being creative partners with God tending the garden of creation (Gen 2 narrative). People are of ultimate value for the Cosmic Other in the life and message of Jesus. People take priority over the cultic values of religion. Healing the sick on a holy Sabbath contrary to the wisdom of the religious elite was obviously right in the mind of Jesus. God, the Cosmic Abba, would have it no other way (Mk 3:1-6; Mt 12:1-14). Within the vision of Jesus, God cared passionately for people, good people and wandering people. The Cosmic Abba waited for wanderers to find their way home and like an anxious father raced through a hillside meadow to embrace a bruised and weary youth (Lk 15:11-32). The Cosmic Abba not only waited but left home, and like a shepherd combed the jagged gullies of the Judean desert seeking the one lost sheep (Lk 15:3-7). The Cosmic Mother spent hours sweeping the house, seeking until she found the treasured coin (Lk 15:8-10).

A Muslim friend and scholar, Dr. G. H. Aasi, after many hours of co-teaching courses in interfaith dialogue, said, "I don't think Muslims have or could ever speak of God searching for sinners.

God, rather, is always the gracious guide who leads us to the straight path and warns us of the consequences of our wrong doings."

The Cosmic Abba Embraces Even the Enemy

Jesus' radical teaching, rejecting the Old Testament "Holy War" theology, is found in Matthew.

"You have heard that it was said, 'You shall love your neighbor and hate your enemy.' But I say to you, Love your enemies and pray for those who persecute you so you may be sons of your Father who is in heaven; for he makes the sun rise on the evil and on the good, and sends rain on the just and on the unjust. For if you love those who love you, what reward have you? Do not even the tax collectors do the same? And if you salute only your brethren, what more are you doing than others? Do not even the Gentiles do the same? You, therefore, must be perfect as your heavenly Father is perfect" (Mt 5:43-48).

The human community is divided by family, clan, tribe, nation, race, gender and religion, but the ultimate division is between friend/neighbor and the enemy. All divisions are erased in Jesus' command for the all-embracing love for the enemy. The feared, the hated, the despised, the unknown, the "evil" ones are embraced with the passionate love of God who as Abba of all embraces even the enemy. Dr. Duane Priebe of Wartburg Theological Seminary always reminds us that whenever we draw a line of separation between "them and us," Jesus is already on the other side of the line!

The Radical Love of the Cosmic Abba
Is Not Locked Up in a Jewish or Christian Box

This radical love also means for Jesus that the saving and healing activity of God is not confined to or circumscribed by those within the "household of faith." Jesus sees God outside his own mission and ministry. In his inaugural sermon (Lk 4:1-44) and to the consternation and rage of the worshipping community Jesus asserts that God uses a Gentile widow to feed Elijah, the prophet, and heals Naaman, the Syrian commander. Jesus portrays the embodiment of compassion for the broken and the enemy in a heretical, non-Jewish Samaritan who takes responsibility for a beaten Jewish traveler on the way to Jericho (Lk 10:29-37). Jesus recognized gratitude in a Samaritan who returned to give thanks for his healing from leprosy (Lk 17:11-19) and faith in a Roman centurion (Lk 7:1-10). Most strikingly, Jesus asserts that salvation is present when citizens of the world's nations and religions compassionately care for the vulnerable "little ones" of a global society (Mt 25:35ff). Jesus was emphatically not a 21st century "exclusivist." One cannot lock God up within a particular religious or denominational box. Jesus is renounced whenever the Abba of Jesus is confined to those who know or follow him.

The Abba's Reign Intends a
Unified and Righteous Filled Human Community

"Your kingdom come, Your will be done on earth as in heaven." Jesus teaches his disciples to pray for the transformation of the earth and challenges people to live as participants in the Reign of God as the will of God molds an earthly communion into a replica of cosmic perfection. Jesus' Sermon on the Mount (Mt 5–7; Lk 6:17-49) is recognized as moral poetry and vision by multitudes outside the Christian community of faith. Jesus in the "Beatitudes" (Mt 5.3-11) sets forth the marks of life within God's transformed world. Humility (poor in spirit); mourning over the brokenness of life; meekness rather than arrogance; hungering and thirsting for righteousness rather than seeking for an abundance of power, wealth, material stuff and sexual satisfaction; mercy rather than retaliation; integrity or pure heartedness rather than duplicity and hypocrisy; peacemaking rather than hate-filled war mongering; the willingness to be tried and tested for the sake of this righteousness—these all are marks of God's new world.

Furthermore, this new world is created primarily for those who have been marginalized or thrown out of the present age and human structures that privilege the rich and powerful. Luke's version of this sermon (Lk 6:12ff) begins:

"Blessed are you poor, for yours is the Kingdom of God. Blessed are you who hunger now, for you will be satisfied. Blessed are you who weep now, for you shall laugh. Blessed are you when men hate you, and when they exclude you and revile you, and cast out your name as evil, on account of the Son of man! Rejoice in that day, and leap for joy, for behold, your reward is great in heaven; for so their fathers did to the prophets."

Here Luke takes us back to Jesus' own focus upon the marginalized and ostracized. For Jesus everyone counts, everyone is invited to God's Messianic banquet. The marginalized often saw and still see their predicament as the absence of God, the silence of God or the judgment of God. Many contemporaries of Jesus saw poverty, tragedy and disease as the judgment of God. Many Christians see God's wrath in every death, failure and disease. Much Muslim theology and also Christian-fundamentalism emphasizes that obedience to Allah brings success in life. Most Buddhists believe that our present lives, whether marked by happiness or horrendous pain, are the direct consequence of our own previous actions through an eternal law designated Karma. If one is born in poverty and disease one receives exactly that which one has earned in the past or previous life. Jesus rejects all of these theological myths that enable the rich and powerful to deal with the poor and diseased with contempt. Jesus simply announces that those despised and rejected ones are God's very top priority. Blessed are the poor, the hungry, the despairing who weep. The Reign of God comes first for you.

We pray, May God's Reign of compassion and righteousness come soon. In the words of the early Jesus community, "Our Lord, come!" (I Cor 16:22).

The Abba's Kingdom is a Seemingly Hidden Kingdom

Jesus was aware of the fact that the Kingdom of God which he announced was not obviously present. Powerful signs were present, indicating that the declaration was not true. Roman power, wealthy landowners, crooked tax collectors, corrupt religious elites exploited the average citizen and crushed the poor. Disease and demons afflicted those broken in body and mind. However, in spite of this striking evidence Jesus said, "The Kingdom of God is approaching and is at hand" (Mk 1:15), the Kingdom of God is at work in the liberation of those afflicted by the demonic (Lk 11:20), the Kingdom of God promised by the prophets is now seen (Lk 10:23-24), the Kingdom of God is not there or here but is already in your midst or within you (Lk 17:21). The Kingdom of God is present, says Jesus, even though seemingly absent. It is like a treasure hidden in a field (Mt 13:44); like leaven hidden within three measures of flour (Mt 13:33); like a tiny mustard seed hidden in the ground (Mt 13:31). Even having observed Jesus' ministry, John the Baptist did not see the reality of the Kingdom (Mt 11:2-17) but questioned Jesus, "Are you he who is to come or do we look for another?" Jesus responded, "If you look carefully you will see signs of the Kingdom's presence as promised by Isaiah" (Is 35:5). "The blind receive their sight and the lame walk, lepers are cleansed and the deaf hear, and the dead are raised up, and the poor have good news preached to them. And blessed is he who takes no offense at me"(Mt 11:5-6).

This seeming hiddenness of the Reign of God is paradoxically encountered as Jesus is crucified. God's reign is thwarted! God is silent! God is not present! God has forsaken Jesus! God is dead! The presence of the abyss and nothingness are a living reality. Incredibly, the resurrection announces that Kingdom defeats are not final. There is hope in the midst of dying and death. God's Reign appears within and reappears beyond defeats, destruction and death.

Jesus as Visionary Prophet of the Kingdom of God: The Birth of an Ethnic-Cultural-Religious Shattering Community

Jesus was born and raised in a pious Jewish family and community living in Galilee of Palestine. He received a childhood education at his mother's feet and in the local synagogue. The New Testament memories indicate that Jesus developed into a skilled an innovative interpreter of the Hebrew scriptures (Lk 4:16 ff.). The Gospel narratives witness to Jesus' thorough acquaintance with Jewish traditions and contemporary Jewish debates. He was recognized as a teacher who spoke with a fresh authentic authority (Mk 1:22, Mt 7:29), and as a skilled debater who left his opponents speechless (Mk 12:34).

Jesus seemed to move effortlessly within his Jewish community knowing its thought and life. He also moved freely distinguishing between that which he thought was superficial and temporary and that which he thought was essential and plumbed the depths of the prophetic faith and wisdom of Israel. When asked what commandment was first of all Jesus replied, "The first is 'Hear O Israel: the Lord our God is one, you shall love the Lord your God with all your heart, and with all your soul, and with all your mind, and with all your strength.' The second is this, 'You shall love your neighbor as yourself.' There is no other commandment greater than these" (Mk 12:29-31). Jesus summary of the law of God draws from the radical roots of Israel's faith expressed in Deuteronomy 6:4-5 and in Leviticus 19:18. It is not only radical in going to the Torah's roots but is also visionary in using this radical summary formulation to distinguish between an essential visionary faith and that which was not necessary to an authentic relationship to God. For example, Mark reports of this freedom of Jesus when he taught his disciples that religious purification rites such as washing the hands were not essential to the human-divine relationship; however, loving and caring for ones' parents was the will of God. Furthermore, dietary laws were not essential because food entered the mouth and passed though the body into the toilet. Food did not enter the heart which was considered to be the center of moral and religious values. However, what comes forth from the heart and destroys life and community such as: adultery, avarice, deceit, envy, slander, pride, these destroy ones' relationship with God and God's people (Mk 7:1-23).

In distinguishing between the essential and the secondary in faith, Jesus planted seeds which would make it possible for an ethnic-cultural-religious shattering community to emerge. The early Jewish Christians found it difficult to distinguish between Jewish religious cultural values and a new value system that identified divine values intended for all humanity. These God-intended values were epitomized in love as compassion and care for all creation and all of God's children. The Book of Acts narrates the struggle of the early Christian Jews as they were challenged to participate in the shattering of their ancient traditions. Acts 10 describes Peter in the process of conversion to a new liberating community. Peter has a vision that there are no clean and unclean animals for God has created them all. Dietary laws are abolished. Furthermore, all humanity is clean by God's own creation. This is affirmed by an incredible event when Gentile/unclean people are baptized with the Spirit before they have entered into the Jewish community through the rite of circumcision. Acts 15 reports a cultural-shattering council as the early Jewish Jesus movement decides that circumcision will no longer be required for the followers of Jesus among the Gentiles.

The radical and visionary interpretation of scripture and tradition by Jesus was a spiritual spark that eventually led to a new ethnic-cultural and religious transcending community which had the possibility of addressing and uniting a common humanity. In this new community there is neither Jew nor Greek, slave nor free, male nor female (Gal 3:28).

This new community could not be bound to a piece of geographical territory because all humanity was to be included even the Roman enemy. God's gift of rain and sunshine fell not only on the Jerusalem temple and the High Priest's Judean vineyard but also upon those of the Roman generals and upon the slaves and free of the Italian peninsula. In the Gospel of John Jesus says to the woman at the well in Samaria, "Woman, believe me the hour is coming when you will worship the Father neither on this mountain nor in Jerusalem....true worshippers will worship in spirit and in truth" (John 4:21-24). No longer will there be a "Holy Land" for the whole earth will be filled with the knowledge of God as the waters cover the sea (Is 11:9).

Most significantly, Jesus' radical and visionary understanding of love makes it impossible to lock God or religion up in a political city, nation or empire. Jesus advocated a Kingdom of God that called for a non-violent participation in the will of God.

> "You have heard that it was said, 'An eye for an eye and a tooth for a tooth.' But I say to you, Do not resist one who is evil. But if any one strikes you on the right cheek, turn to him the other also;... and if any one forces you to go one mile, go with him two miles...You have heard that it was said, 'You shall love your neighbor and hate your enemy.' But I say to you, Love your enemies and pray for those who persecute you, so that you may be sons of your Father who is in heaven; for he makes his sun rise on the evil and on the good. And sends rain on the just and the unjust" (Matthew 5:38-45).

A new ethnic-cultural-religious-transcending community molded by Jesus' non-violent coming of the Kingdom of God will not be locked up in a political city, nation or empire because political units use, need and demand violent power to exist. Police and armies are essential to their existence. From the perspective of Jesus, the coming of God's Kingdom, the vision of God's future will not be imposed by nor limited by the power of armed men and political submission. This Kingdom will penetrate ethnic-cultural-religious walls and permeate the totality of life as leaven in a loaf (Mt 13:33), salt in a soup (Mt 5:13) and light in the darkness (Mt 5:14).

In Jesus' day, Palestine was a hotbed of Jewish terrorism and revolution. Jewish zealots demanded that since Israel had only God as King all Roman powers loyal to Caesar were to be driven from the Holy Land. A few decades after Jesus' crucifixion, the Jewish people revolted against Rome demanding their freedom. The revolution was crushed in 70 C.E. and again in 135 C.E. Jerusalem was leveled as a field and the inhabitants were either killed or deported.

Jesus' teachings of love for the enemy and his call to cooperate with the occupying troops (Mt 5:41) were a direct rejection of the militant zealot revolutionaries. Jesus called for a radically new engagement with the enemy marked by vulnerable, non-violent compassion. He warned that the Jewish revolutionary movement would culminate in disaster (Lk 19:41-44) which it did. Tragically Jesus' crucifixion at the hands of the Roman authorities was triggered by his popularity which was seen as a political threat to the Pax Romana.

This radical and visionary approach of Jesus to Jewish Law and Tradition led to a division (one of many) within the Jewish community. His distinctions between that which was primary and secondary placed him at odds with many Pharisees. His call for non-violence placed him in opposition to the political revolutionaries (Zealots and some Pharisees. The revolt of 130-135 was authorized by the lead Rabbi Akiba who volunteered as the armor-bearer of the Zealot and Messianic fighter, Bar Kochba.) Jesus compassionate vision of the Reign of God critiqued all those priests who commercialized worship in the Holy Temple. His vision came to be embodied in a new community of faith that ultimately split with its Jewish cultural roots. Unfortunately much of the Christian community has since also split with its Jesus roots.

It has often been noted that the mission of Jesus focused upon Jews and not Gentiles. The previous discussion, I believe, indicates why. Jesus saw himself as a member of the community of Israel called by God to be a light to the nations (Is 48/49, Mt 5) and salt for the earth. However, with John the Baptist he was aware that Israel's leadership had lost its way—the light had gone out; the salt had lost its savor and could be thrown out. Therefore, John and Jesus cried, "Repent, for the Reign of God is drawing near!" God calls for a renewed people with lanterns lighted, a salt and leaven people permeating and transforming the world, creating a new "People of God"—ethnically, culturally and religiously transformed.

Jesus as the Resurrected Messiah

The early followers of Jesus were convinced that the crucifixion was not the end of his life or work. He was killed by Roman legions but death did not hold him. He lived; they met him; his baptism into the reality of God's Spirit was a power which transformed and motivated their lives. During the pre-Golgotha ministry of Jesus his followers had identified him as a prophet, the prophet, the Son of David and a New Israel and the Messiah of God's Kingdom. However, his death had shattered all of those dreams.

Their resurrection faith rekindled these hopes and dreams. Jesus now was the living and awaited Messiah, the bearer of God's Kingdom and the hope of prophetic dreams being fulfilled. Jesus as Messiah embodied the coming Kingdom of God; he concretized the heavenly will of God as the will of God on earth (The Lord's Prayer). Soon Christians were saying that the Word of God (the Logos of God) was embodied in the Galilean carpenter and prophet. This faith therefore trusted that which was seen, heard and touched in Jesus expressed the very reality of God's presence and reign. Creative, nurturing, transforming love met in Jesus expressed the eternal reality of God. The Word of God became flesh (John 1.14). Central to this new message was the fact that Jesus crucified was also Jesus risen. The encounter with Jesus beginning in Galilee continued with a risen reality—Jesus the Messiah who sits at the right hand of God. However, this risen Christ still bore the marks of the cross (John 20:26-28).

The Apostle Paul illustrates this post-Easter encounter with Jesus. Paul had begun his religious career as Saul, a highly trained Pharisee. When he first heard reports of Jesus and his followers he had concluded that they were a dangerous heretical cult that threatened the true faith of Israel. Finally Saul's reading of the Sacred Text led him to the conclusion that God had cursed Jesus as a betrayer of the faith (Gal 3:13-14). This conviction was based on his reading of Deuteronomy 21:23: "Cursed be everyone who hangs on a tree."

Terrified by the possibility of the loss of God's truth to heresy, Saul with other colleagues initiated a persecution of Jesus disciples. They had them imprisoned and put to death (Acts 7.54-60). This fiery persecution began in Jerusalem and then moved to Damascus in Syria. Saul was sent to Damascus to carry out the attack on the early Jesus people (Acts 9:22,26). The Jesus movement in the name of God had to be stopped even if it meant imprisonment and death to a few misguided religious fanatics. It was in the midst of Saul's attack on Jesus' people that Saul met Jesus.

"Thus I journeyed to Damascus with the authority and commission of the chief priests. At midday, O king, I saw on the way a light from heaven, brighter than the sun, shining around me and those who journeyed with me. And when we had all fallen to the ground, I heard a voice saying to me in the Hebrew language, 'Saul, Saul, why do you persecute me? It hurts you to kick against the goads.' And I said, 'Who are you, Lord?' And the Lord said, 'I am Jesus whom you are persecuting. But rise and stand upon your feet; for I have appeared to you for this purpose, to appoint you to serve and bear witness to the things in which you have seen me and to those in which I will appear to you, delivering you from the people and from the Gentiles – to whom I send you to open their eyes, that they may turn from darkness to light and from the power of Satan to God, that they may receive forgiveness of sins and a place among those who are sanctified by faith in me'" (Acts 26:12-18).

It was this encounter with the crucified and resurrected Christ that transformed Saul's life. This experience with the risen Lord transformed his understanding of his relationship with God. From his letters we know that as a Pharisee Saul believed that his relationship with God was grounded in his obedience to the Law of God. Salvation depended on his faithful obedience (Galatians and Romans). Now Saul was confronted with Jesus, right in the middle of his attack upon Jesus' people. Jesus met him and called him, Paul, to discipleship. Paul never forgot that, and at the heart of his message was this confession: "While I was a sinner Christ called me." "While we were yet sinners Christ died for us" (Rom 5:6-11). Jesus was cursed, but for us (Gal 3:13).

This Pauline experience of the risen Christ has become a model for Christian conversion, rebirth. "Lord, I am a sinner; have mercy on me." This confession is followed by trust in Jesus' words, "Your sins are forgiven. Go in peace! I died that you might live!" Paul spoke of this gift of God as grace, an unconditional love offered to sinners if they will simply receive the gift. The renowned 20th century theologian, Paul Tillich, spoke of this gift as simply acceptance of one's unconditional divine acceptance.

This book, *Jesus, the Word, and the Way of the Cross*, is rooted in this Pauline experience. However, it is also rooted in early Christian memories of Jesus' pre-crucifixion ministry. His life and mission enables us to more fully grasp the reality of Jesus as the crucified and risen Christ.

Costly Love—Costly Discipleship

God's love is revealed and active in the crucifixion of Jesus as he prophetically acts, speaks and as he is killed by those he infuriated. In this event, God declares that divine love is self-giving, suffering, all-embracing and vulnerable even to death. God in love is vulnerable unto death in our midst; therefore, God's love is costly. "You know that you were ransomed from the futile ways inherited from your ancestors, not by perishable things like silver and gold, but with the precious blood of Christ" (1 Pt 1:18-19b).

It is essential in our time and for our task that the gospel message centered in God's costly love be found in Jesus' paradoxical lordship. The early Christians confessed that the one who was exalted to the right hand of God and before whom every knee will bow is the one who emptied himself, took the form of a servant and became obedient even to death on the cross (Phil 2:5-11). The New Testament proclaims repeatedly that the risen Son of the living God is the one who, as suffering servant, went through a messianic struggle, death and hell for the world's sake. There is the awesome wonder that he who was rich became poor (2 Cor 8:9); that the Word of God became flesh and lived among us (John 1:14); that the Lord washed his disciples' feet (John 13); that the Christ hung in the darkness of Calvary and died for the sins of the world (John 1:29).

The incredible, awesome wonder of the gospel is that God, the Creator, Molder and Future of the universe, was and is concretized among us as a humble, suffering servant who willingly dies in God's mission for the world. God has been here but not as we expected. Power appeared in seeming weakness, in compassion, service and death. God has been identified as the vulnerable one in our midst. The gospel was and is costly.

It is absolutely essential that we proclaim a gospel shaped by the Jesus crucified rather than a message shaped by our cultural values and norms. It is essential that it is Jesus crucified, not ourselves, who defines God and the mission of God. The marks of divine love enfleshed in Jesus are not self-serving but self-giving and sacrifice for others; not indifference and distance but compassion as suffering-with-love; not domineering arrogance but humble servanthood; not power and invincibility but vulnerability. That is incredible costly love. Nail-pierced hands and a wounded side are permanent marks of the risen one (John 20). The Christ we follow did not and does not come as over-powering king but as compassionate, suffering servant who dies for the healing of the nations (Is 42, 49, 53). In contrast to our cultural values and norms, the gospel message is cruciform. Salvation is rooted in the vulnerable, costly love of God.

Also of primary significance is the fact that the messengers proclaiming the gospel be understood as participants in the mission of God incarnate in Jesus crucified. Not only our message must be formed and informed by the cross, but our style and form of presence in the world must be formed by the cross. "Take up your cross and follow me!" (Mk 8:31ff). Costly grace calls forth costly discipleship. The Asian scholar, Choan-Seng Song, addressing the same missiological issue, asserts that many within the missionary movement were not able to distinguish between the brutal political power of the West and the saving power of love's vulnerability concretized in Jesus.

> How different is this God of the pompous church and militant missions from the God of the cross! The God we encounter in Jesus on the cross is powerless and helpless. In this vast and rich universe, God has nothing to support Jesus but the two cruel wooden beams representing pain, shame and suffering. But this is precisely the God who has power to save the world.[3]

The followers of Jesus have been grasped by a cruciform gospel, by incredible costly love. We have been called to a cruciform style of mission and ministry, costly discipleship. What are the implications of a theology of Jesus and the cross for our proclamation and understanding of the gospel, and for our understanding of our discipleship? What are the consequences of being called to speak and act in his name?

The Centrality of the Cross and the New Testament

The mission of God has been viewed and understood from a variety of perspectives. The church's participation in the mission of God has been rooted in: the apostolic imperative, "Go and make disciples of all nations" (Mt 28:20);[4] the church's pentecostal empowerment;[5] the trinitarian creedal formulation;[6] the biblical understanding of the kingdom of God;[7] and others. Each of these studies begins from a particular viewpoint and attempts to explore the rich dimensions of the mission of God from that perspective.

This particular missiological exploration begins by focusing upon Jesus as the crucified and from that viewpoint attempts to articulate the implications of this approach for understanding the mission of God and God's missioning people. The decision to begin with Jesus and the cross is not arbitrary. As noted earlier, a focus upon the Cosmic Crucified as the presence and action of the suffering God speaks powerfully today both to Christians witnessing among Muslims and Buddhists as well as to Muslims and Buddhists.

Of greater weight is the biblical fact that the cross is central to the New Testament's understanding of the gospel.

The death of Jesus is central to the New Testament. Passion narratives receive major emphases in the Gospels. The epistles of the New Testament often explore the depths of the faith from the perspective of the crucified and risen Lord. The awe and wonder of the early church are expressed by Paul, "While we were still weak [sinners], at the right time Christ died for the ungodly" (Rom 5:6). "Therefore, I decided to know nothing among you except Jesus Christ, and him crucified" (1 Cor 2:2). It is obvious that if Jesus had been crucified and remained dead, the disciples would have continued to say, "But we had hoped that he was the one to redeem Israel" (Lk 24:21). The Resurrection, however, became an experienced fact. Jesus, the crucified, was seen, recognized and known as risen. The Apostolic witness centered in these words, "The Lord has risen indeed, and he has appeared to Simon!" (Lk 24:34); to Mary (John 20:1-18); to the 12, to 500, to James, to all the apostles, to Paul (1 Cor 15:1-8). God had raised him and Jesus was proclaimed as the Cosmic Crucified who now poured out the power of the Spirit upon his disciples. That was and is awesome joy. C. S. Song writes:

> Theology should be an ode of love. . . . Theology without the pain and agony of love is not theology. It is a make-believe monologue directed to no one but itself. Nor is theology without joy and exultation true theology. It is an endlessly dull discourse that puts to sleep not only the audience, but the speakers themselves. Such a theology has nothing to do with the God of the Christian Bible who creates the world and redeems it in passionate love.[8]

Chapter 2

Jesus and the Cross: God's Radical Mission Identified

God's radical mission comes to expression in the life, work and violent death of Jesus. This volume integrates the mission and crucifixion of Jesus in order to enable his death to explore the meaning of his life and to allow his life to interpret the meaning of his death. It is hoped that this approach to Jesus and the cross will give new insights into the reality of our faith and the radicality of God's mission, particularly in our engagement with Muslims and Buddhists.

In seeking to understand Jesus and the cross I present three dimensions of God's mission which are revealed and concretized in Jesus:

1. That God intends and struggles for the transformation of all of life. Jesus as prophet of God's transforming Kingdom is opposed and rejected by destructive powers. It is this struggle between the Kingdom of God and the kingdom of darkness that results in Jesus being nailed to the cross

2. That God in transforming the world is present and vulnerable among us in Jesus' life and ministry. The vulnerability of God's love is epitomized in Jesus' crucifixion. This is what makes reconciliation with God possible.

3. That God is continually passionately present within human life which is marked by brokenness, pain and suffering.

It is hoped that the presentation will clarify who we are and what we are called to be as disciples of the crucified Prince of Peace.

Jesus Crucified: the Messianic Struggle for Life in the Midst of Death

Gustav Aulen in his book, *Christus Victor*, interprets Jesus' death and resurrection in cosmic, dualistic terms.[9] Jesus Christ dies in a cosmic battle between the Kingdom of God and the demonic "principalities and powers." Jesus' death and resurrection are God's ultimate triumph over the powers of sin, death and the devil. It is essential to reclaim this conflict-victory theme for an understanding of the totality of God's saving, atoning work; however, the conflict-victory theme must be radically interpreted in the light of Jesus crucified. The nature of the combat must be seen in Jesus as the powerful yet vulnerable-to-death prophet. The conflict-victory theme can never be understood in terms of our contemporary understanding of might and power nor our seeming eternal quest for invulnerability. Only the life and death of Jesus defines the conflict and the power. The conflict is a struggle that God's *will* might be done on earth even as it is done in heaven. The power is self-giving, serving love, which is willing to be vulnerable to death in order that newness of life might be realized.

The New Testament document Luke-Acts describes the cosmic duel in Kingdom and Spirit terms. Jesus announced the nearness and arrival of the promised reign/kingdom of God. The prophetic promises of Isaiah are fulfilled (Lk 4:18-21, 7:22-23); the disciples have seen what prophets and kings had longed to see (Lk 10:23); the kingdom's power sets captives free (Lk 11:20); and a new age of the kingdom had dawned (Lk 16:16) and was already in the midst of them (Lk 17:20-21). The arrival of God's kingdom, empowered by the Spirit of God (Jesus' birth, Lk 1:35; baptism, Lk 3:21-22; ministry, Lk 4:18) brought kingdom life and light into the realm of death and darkness. The encounter between the kingdom and the satanic powers (Lk 11:14-23) resulted in the ultimate combat between life and death. The cosmic triumph of God over sin, death and the devil cost Jesus' life. He hung on Golgotha in the darkness and the wind. On the third day God raised Jesus from the dead. The risen crucified manifests God's victory over sin and death (Acts 2)!

Aulen sees Martin Luther as a primary interpreter of this "classical" view of cosmic conflict and victory in Jesus Christ.[10] In the great Reformation hymn, Luther wrote:

> A mighty fortress is our God,
> A sword and shield victorious;
> He breaks the cruel oppressor's rod
> And wins salvation glorious.
> The old satanic foe
> Has sworn to work us woe!

With craft and dreadful might
    He arms himself to fight.
On earth he has no equal.

No strength of ours can match his might!
    We would be lost, rejected.
But now a champion comes to fight,
    Whom God himself elected.
You ask who this may be?
    The Lord of hosts is he!
Christ Jesus, mighty Lord,
    God's only Son, adored.
He holds the field victorious.[11]

In *Luther and Liberation: A Latin American Perspective*[12] Walter Altmann asserts in a similar way that Luther's Christology is dynamic and combative:

> This is especially clear when his theology concentrates on the cross, the point of confluence in the historical and cosmic battle between evil and righteousness, curse and blessing, and death and life. Here, there is no defeated resignation but rather shared and redemptive suffering. The dead Jesus of popular Latin American veneration may be the expression of resigned and impotent suffering (and may also be an image that helps people survive under oppression), but Christ-crucified, as interpreted by Luther, is divine love's combatant. His cross is not defeat, but rather the victorious culmination of an all-out battle. Hence, Christus victor—victorious Christ. [13]

Then Altmann writes, "Throughout the course of the history of the Lutheran church, the combative aspect has been forgotten along with the necessity of following Jesus Christ in his path, of joining Jesus Christ in his kenosis, his emptying out."[14] Altmann, who has deep roots within the Lutheran tradition, has been deeply influenced by his Latin American context, marked by poverty and oppression, and shares deeply in the Latin American churches' struggle to relate the gospel of Jesus Christ to that situation. With other Latin American theologians, Altmann understands Jesus' crucifixion as the outcome of a liberation struggle waged between Jesus and his religious and political contemporaries. However, this historical conflict is rooted in the cosmic conflict between the kingdom of God and the powers of darkness.[15]

The Catholic theologian Leonardo Boff writes:

Through his life and message, Jesus, acting in the name of God, strove to inculcate in human beings a spirit that would never cause crosses for others; and now he himself hangs on a cross. His cross is not the result of an arbitrary whim on God's part. It results from the way in which the world is organized. Sinfully closed in upon itself, the world rejected the God of Jesus and eliminated Jesus himself. The execution of Jesus is the greatest sin ever committed because it stands in opposition to God's will, which is to establish the Kingdom in the midst of the creation.[16]

God or the kingdom of God was embodied in Jesus. The powers of darkness were embodied in priests, scholars, governors, kings and throngs. Boff writes, "They were actors in a drama that went much deeper than they themselves. The real protagonists were the Evil One and the sin of the world; they were the ones ultimately responsible for Jesus' death."[17] Jesus as bearer of the kingdom preached good news to the poor, proclaimed forgiveness to the damned, healed the sick, liberated the possessed. However, Jesus' messianic ministry enraged the religious and scholarly elite and aroused the hostility of the political powers. In other words, it was Jesus' struggle to bring God's life-giving kingdom into the midst of death that infuriated those who embodied the powers of darkness: the powers of religious, social, economic, and political oppression.

There were specific historical reasons why Jesus battled the powers of darkness that ruled Galilee and Judea, and there were specific historical reasons why Jesus was nailed to a cross. On behalf of the kingdom's struggle for life, Jesus prophetically challenged the faith, values, and traditions of his contemporaries. "Though Jesus was more than a prophet, it was his prophetic call to change that caused his death."[18] It was the struggle for kingdom-life and Jesus' prophetic challenge of the voices of darkness that hung Jesus in the dust and the wind. If we are to witness to Jesus Christ crucified, it is essential that we explore the relationship between Jesus' death at the hands of his enemies and Jesus' struggle on behalf of God's life-giving kingdom.[19]

We will explore Jesus' prophetic ministry in some detail because our Muslim and Buddhist friends are often fascinated by Jesus' life and mission. They may have absolutely no interest in Augustine, Thomas Aquinas, Luther or Calvin, but they often desire "to see

Jesus," and it is in Jesus that they will see the presence and action of the kingdom of God as God contests with the powers of darkness. This missiology of Jesus and the cross places Jesus' prophetic ministry of the approaching kingdom of God in an integral relationship to the cross and God's vulnerability unto death for the ungodly concretized in Jesus.

Life for the Damned

Jesus' unconditional, self-giving, seeking love for those stigmatized as lost or "damned"; Jesus' willingness to converse and eat with them; and his freedom to announce grace and forgiveness in their midst astounded Jesus' contemporaries. It is not surprising that the Gospel of Luke concludes:

> "Thus it is written, that the Messiah is to suffer and to rise from the dead on the third day, and that repentance and forgiveness of sins is to be proclaimed in his name to all nations." (Lk 24:46-47)

Some of Jesus' contemporaries were not only astounded but were appalled and infuriated by Jesus' words and actions. Jesus violated and desecrated their understanding of God's will and intended order for God's people.

There seems to be a universal principle at work within religious people of the world. They are always drawing circles around God. There are those inside the circle named the elect, the called, the blessed, the saved of God, and there are those outside the circle named the non-elected, those who are outside the blessing and salvation of God, the damned. Jesus makes it very clear that when religious people draw circles demarking insiders and outsiders in terms of moral standards, religious rectitude, race, or sex, one can always know that Jesus will be on the other side of the line, insisting that God wills in love to embrace the whole human community.[20]

In *Jesus: A New Vision*, Marcus Borg describes what he considers to be the historical and sociological origins of this religious tendency among Jesus' contemporaries. He believes that many within the Jewish community saw their religious traditions and values being threatened by Hellenistic culture and Roman political power. In order to prevent the destruction of their own way of life, they developed what Borg designates "the politics of holiness," which emphasized "God was holy and Israel was to be holy."[21] The Pharisees were leading advocates of this holiness movement focusing on religious and ritual purity and tithing. Failure to live in accordance with holiness norms resulted in ostracism, and "the major vehicle of social and religious ostracism was the refusal of table fellowship."[22] In contrast to the "politics of holiness," Borg sees Jesus develop the "politics of compassion" marked by, among other things, banqueting with outcasts, association with women, good news for the poor and peace advocacy within a revolutionary hate environment.[23] An awareness of these universal and particular holiness norms are essential as one attempts to understand the radical message and mission of Jesus and the violent opposition Jesus eventually aroused.

Luke collects a number of stories and parables of Jesus that reflect Jesus' radical grace and the criticism and resentment Jesus' ministry began to arouse. There is the "woman of the city, who was a sinner," who wept at Jesus' feet, anointing Jesus' feet with oil (Lk 7:36-50). This took place as Jesus was dining in the home of a Pharisee named Simon. Imagine what brought this woman into the midst of the religious authorities who despised her. Could it have been that Jesus was the first person who spoke of God who also had spoken to her–talked to her as if she were someone of value, someone for whom God cared? Might she have heard him tell the parable of the prodigal son? (Lk 15:11-24) Whatever brought her there, the miracle of the story is that she knew that she could trust Jesus, that Jesus would not ridicule her and send her away. In gratitude she wept at his feet, and she heard him say, "Your sins are forgiven; go in peace." That is bringing life into the midst of death, life to the damned.

Jesus' saving action and words were immediately contested. The Pharisees contended that a man of God, a prophet, would recognize what sort of woman this was touching him (Lk 7:39). People of God, people set apart for that which is holy, were not to touch, flesh against flesh, those who had defiled themselves in sin. To Jesus she was not the profaned, the sinner, the damned; she was the wayward child of God who had come home, one for whom the Father had wept and of whom he had dreamed, one who was to be swept into God's open and embracing arms. To many of the Pharisees she was an irresponsible and degenerate woman who would not experience the presence and forgiveness of God.

Luke in chapter 19 tells the story of Zacchaeus, the crooked tax collector and political collaborator from Jericho (Lk l9:1-10). Zacchaeus was rich, despised by the patriotic Jewish community for both his greed and his willingness to cooperate with the Roman invaders and by the religious community because of failure to live by its holiness code. Perhaps he despised himself as thoroughly as did the patriotic and religious community. Something compelled him to look for Jesus, and he was filled with joy when Jesus said that he wanted to spend the day with him. There was an immediate reaction within the crowd. "They all murmured, 'He has gone in to be the guest of one who is a sinner.'" Jesus said, "He too is a son of Abraham."

Like Matthew and Mark, Luke also relates how Jesus called Levi, a tax collector, to be his disciple (Lk 5:27-32). Levi gave a banquet attended by a large crowd of tax collectors and others sitting at the table. Again the Pharisees and Scribes were complaining, "Why do you eat and drink with the tax collectors and sinners?" Jesus' practice of banqueting with sinners led to the accusation that he was "a glutton and drunkard, a friend of tax collectors and sinners" (Lk 7:34). Jesus responded to the questions and charges by saying he had come to seek the lost (Lk 19:10), to call sinners to repentance (Lk 5:32), to announce the forgiveness of God (Lk 7:47). Jesus insisted that his message and mission was molded by God and necessary to kingdom-life.

Jesus asserted that God was with those relegated to "the damned" and that God's incomprehensible forgiveness was there. Outside the temple, the synagogue, the authoritarian ministry, the traditional religious community, God was there sharing the pain of the ostracized, crossing lines and destroying walls. Jesus defended his evangelical witness, asserting that God, like a shepherd, seeks lost sinners (Lk 15:3-7) and God, like a woman overwhelmed with the excitement of finding one lost coin from her wedding dowry, rejoices when one lost sinner is found (Lk 15:8-10). Jesus announced that a tax collector, defiled, lost and "damned," was loved and forgiven/justified while weeping before God alone in the temple (Lk 18:9-14). This proclamation was grace for the damned. It was a struggle for life in the midst of death. It resulted in a costly conflict for which Jesus would finally lose his life. Oppressive religious traditions and hierarchical authorities were not about to step aside without a struggle. They would eventually insist that this false messianic prophet must die, and Jesus, walking the vulnerable way required by his Father in heaven, would hang outside the walls of the holy city.

Unconditional grace and forgiveness, rooted in the pain-love of God, are at the heart of the gospel. They are at the heart of the proclamation that Jesus is the Cosmic Crucified; they were at the heart of Jesus' own kingdom message and mission. This gospel must be our gospel!

> But God, who is rich in mercy, out of the great love with which he loved us even when we were dead through our trespasses, made us alive together with Christ—by grace you have been saved—. . . and this is not your own doing; it is the gift of God (Eph 2:4-10).

This message astounded Jesus' contemporaries. Some received it with awe-filled joy; others resented the seeming "cheap and unjust grace" (Mt 20:1-16). The message still astounds us and often is limited by us as we prescribe the limits of God's costly pain-love. As we converse with Muslims and Buddhists we should not be surprised that we often find the same skepticism about an understanding of God which insists that justice must be understood within the context of God's unconditional suffering love rather than seeing compassion through the lens of justice.

Good News to the Poor

In the Gospel of Luke, Jesus began his ministry with the words:

> "The Spirit of the Lord is upon me, because he has anointed me to bring good news to the poor. He has sent me to proclaim release to the captives and recovery of sight to the blind, to let the oppressed go free, to proclaim the year of the Lord's favor" (Lk 4:18-19).

This messianic passage from Isaiah 61, which Jesus says is fulfilled in his ministry, begins with the announcement that good news is preached to the poor. I believe many of us are beginning to realize what this means—why it is incredibly good news!

Human existence is marked by suffering and death. Often those who experience most deeply the tragic pain of life are those who live in poverty and under oppression. Those who live in poverty often experience hunger. They give birth to children only to see them grow malnourished and subject to disease. They see opportunities for themselves and their children limited by their financial resources or society's prejudices. They experience the cold of winter without sufficient fuel. They often leave their homes and families in order to earn wages to feed and clothe their families. They experience the loneliness of human isolation, whether it be as blind beggars on the streets of Calcutta or refugees on the Somalian desert. They are usually the victims of economic and political warfare. They are the ones exploited by social-political structures grounded in greed and prejudice. They are the ones who are ignored, forgotten, ridiculed, and abused by the world's rich and powerful. They are the ones who often conclude that God has also forgotten them. Everything surrounding people living in poverty and under oppression suggests "God is not with you! God is not here! If God lives, God has forgotten you, ignores you—or even worse, God is punishing you!"

There seems to be something universal about what Hindu people call the law of *karma*. *Karma* means that for every human action, there is a cosmic reaction. Evil actions always result in cosmic judgment. Good actions always result in cosmic reward. This karmic law is seen working through the principle of reincarnation. If one is living in poverty or afflicted by leprosy, one knows that one is experiencing the consequences of evil actions performed in a previous existence. If one lives in health and prosperity, one lives with the consequences of previous good actions. One always knows that one is getting exactly what one deserves.

Jesus' contemporaries had similar thoughts within their religious culture. When Jesus' disciples saw a blind man, they asked, "Who sinned, this man or his parents?" (John 9:2). When a tower of Siloam fell upon people, Jesus' contemporaries immediately assumed that they were greater sinners than those who had been spared (Lk 13:1-5). Likewise, Jesus' contemporaries assumed that health and wealth were a sign of God's blessing. Jesus left his disciples astounded when he said that it was practically impossible for a rich man to be saved. Who then, they asked can possibly be saved? (Mk 10:17-27). Millions of people still accept the idea that poverty and oppression are God's punishment for sin, while wealth is God's reward for righteousness.[24] In its most blatant form this idea was expounded by South African white Christians who taught that black people were cursed by God and intended to be the servants of white people until the close of history. The Reverend Zephania Kameeta, a black Namibian pastor, who now serves as Bishop of his church, put that curse in contemporary language with the words, "We have been taught all our lives that we are God's mistake."

Millions of people not only suffer and die in poverty and under oppression, but they suffer and die believing that their poverty not only signifies the absence of God and the silence of God, but possibly, the judgment of God. Into that tragic pain-filled world

Jesus comes to share and bear the world's suffering. He announces the arrival and presence of the kingdom of God in himself (Lk 10:23-24; 11:20; 17:21), and he promises that the kingdom of God comes to turn the world upside down. Contrary to all the signs which might indicate that the poor and oppressed have been forgotten or condemned Jesus promises:

> "Blessed are you who are poor, for yours is the kingdom of God. Blessed are you who are hungry now, for you will be filled. Blessed are you who weep now, for you will laugh" (Lk 6:20-21).

Strange as it might seem, this promise of life for the poor was one of the factors that contributed to the death of Jesus. Jesus' contemporary critics insisted that poverty, sickness, and death were signs of God's judgment. Jesus contradicted that. They also believed that health and prosperity were signs of their right (inside) relationship with God. Jesus vehemently denied that also. To the contrary, Jesus cried:

> "Woe to you who are rich, for you have received your consolation. Woe to you who are full now, for you will be hungry. Woe to you who are laughing now, for you will mourn and weep" (Lk 6:24-25).

Health and wealth were no assurance of God's blessing. Instead, Jesus saw them as likely signs that something was tragically wrong in human life (Lk 16:19-31). Jesus saw in wealth the possibility that humanity might place their ultimate confidence in wealth rather than God (Lk 12:13-21). He also saw wealth as a God-given resource to be shared with all humanity, particularly the poor. Jesus constantly challenged people of wealth to share God's resources of which they were stewards or to be judged as those outside the kingdom of God (Mt 25:31-46; Mk 10:17-27; Lk 12:32-34; 14:12-14; 19:1-10). Jesus saw the wealthy torn between God and their wealth, and he said, "You cannot serve God and wealth" (Lk 16:13). Luke then comments, "The Pharisees, who were lovers of money, heard all this, and they ridiculed him." Knowing that their ridicule hid their inner rebellion Jesus replied, "You are those who justify yourselves in the sight of others; but God knows your hearts; for what is prized by human beings is an abomination in the sight of God" (Lk 16:14-15). No doubt the combat that hung Jesus in the dust and the wind was vigorously in process.

One of the theological miracles of the late twentieth century is the rediscovery of the biblical witness to God's particular concern for the poor and oppressed, "the preferential option for the poor."[25] It is not surprising that it was the Christian community living in poverty and under oppression that rediscovered this basic biblical motif. Persons living within poverty and oppression read the Bible with different eyes from most of us. Prophetic visions of justice, comfort for the oppressed, denunciations of tyranny normally missed by comfortable Christians of affluent societies leap from the page when read by Christians of Korea, India, Sudan, South Africa, and Latin America.

It is the poor and oppressed who are comforted and empowered by Jesus' blessings and woes. They hear from the prophets and the Risen One that the political and economic forces that crush their lives are not the instruments of God. They are, rather, demonic structures that lie under the judgment of God. It is Jesus who promises that God's kingdom, contrary to all visible signs, has already grasped the poor, and God's future is God's gift to them. This gospel empowers people crushed by historical realities to live in God's marvelous light. People who have had their faces pushed into the dust and have been told that they are society's nobodies are suddenly, in Christ, somebody unique and special, the children of God! People who have questioned the value of their own existence suddenly in faith know themselves to be created in the image of God with value and gifts they have never dreamed of. Dalit theology, an Indian theology of the "crushed ones" or outcasts, emphasizes Hosea's theme, "Once you were no people of mine, now you are my people, children of the living God"(Hos 2:23). Dalit theology focuses on every human being as created in the image of God and therefore having divine value and potential gifts. It is this same liberating theme that has been seen by women who read the Bible with new eyes. Repentance from this perspective can been seen as dying to one's old self which denies one's God-given value and potential in order to be raised to a new empowered life of discipleship by the power of the gospel and the Holy Spirit. In the words of Desmond Tutu, this biblical faith, rediscovered by the world's marginalized, empowers the oppressed to stop shuffling their feet in the presence of the powerful and "look the chap in the eye and speak face to face."[26]

Out of that experience giants in the faith arise: persons who in Jesus' name continue his prophetic ministry; persons who are ridiculed, imprisoned, and tortured for righteousness' sake; persons who arise every morning to walk in Christ's way even though it may mean death; persons whom we must listen to and know in order that we might once again hear the call of Jesus to discipleship and be grasped by the power of his Spirit.

Healing the Sick and Liberating the Oppressed

Jesus' life-giving ministry touched the blind, the lame, the lepers, the deaf, the possessed, and the dead. Jesus gave them sight, made them walk, cleansed their skin, opened their eyes, unstopped their ears. His healing-liberating ministry set them free and gave them life. Jesus claimed that these were signs that the kingdom of God and God's Messiah were here (Lk 7:22; Is 29:18-19; 35:5-6) and the demonic powers were being deposed (Lk 11:14-23). Human lives were being healed, human bodies were being transformed, and the Spirit of God was the energizing power in the midst of that (Acts 10:38). Kingdom-life appeared in the midst of death. Jesus announced that the coming and the presence of God's kingdom was the fulfillment of the prophetic dreams of Israel. Prophets had dreamed that one day God would do a "new thing." The whole of creation would be restored (Is 11:1-9). Isaiah described this restored world:

> Then the eyes of the blind shall be opened, and the ears of the deaf unstopped; then the lame shall leap like a deer, and the tongue of the speechless sing for joy. For waters shall break forth in the wilderness, and streams in the desert.(Is 35:5-7).

Jesus announced that God had begun to do "a new thing." "Blessed are your eyes," said Jesus, for "many prophets and kings desired to see what you see, and did not see it" (Lk 10:23-24). The kingdom of God had been inaugurated.

The messianic dream was being fulfilled. Total fulfillment was still a future dream; however, the mustard seed had been planted, and the leaven was already at work in the loaf (Lk 13:18-21). The blind saw, the deaf heard, the poor had good news preached to them.

The healing-liberating ministry of Jesus was a mark of God's work of restoration and re-creation. God intends to transform the whole of creation—human bodies and minds as well as their souls. It is essential to see that Jesus' miracles and exorcisms were not just religious sideshows that somehow authenticated his message of forgiveness and the promise of eternal life. They were an essential part of Jesus' mission, which proclaimed God's presence and saving action in words of truth, healing of re-creation, and liberation of the demonically oppressed.

Participation in the mission of the crucified Jesus means that witness to the gospel takes the totality of human lives in all their relationships with utmost seriousness. If one is to witness to the Jesus of Scripture in the ghettos of the nations, one must be concerned about people's bodies—in other words, their health, their wages, their families, their contracts, as well as their personal life with God.

This dimension of Jesus' ministry is rooted in the Christian conviction that the God and Father of Jesus the Christ is the creator of the heavens and the earth. Within the silence of eternity God speaks, and there is light and reality. God speaks, creation is, and it is good! Within the chaos of darkness there is life and order and truth. Humanity in rebellion distorts that beauty of life, which in God's eyes is good; however, the Bible insists that within the suffering and brokenness of life there are signs of God's original creativity, remnants of that which is good. Furthermore, the creative and redemptive power of God incarnate in the Cosmic Crucified continues to bring light and creativity into the darkness and death, and faith trusts that there will be one day a new heaven and a new earth. "God himself will be with them; he will wipe every tear from their eyes. Death will be no more" (Rev 21:3-4).

Paradoxically, it was the healing ministry of Jesus that once again brought Jesus into conflict with the religious establishment of his day. The conflict is illustrated by an incident in a synagogue on a Sabbath (Mk 3:1-6). A man with a withered hand appeared. Jesus' critics watched carefully to see whether Jesus would heal him on this holy day. The context suggests that Jesus had healed on Sabbath days in the past. Sharp lines were drawn between Jesus and his opponents. The religious authorities insisted that the Sabbath day was a holy day on which work should not be done. Had not God said on the Sabbath you shall do no work? (Ex 20:8-11). According to the hierarchy, priority had to be placed on religious tradition and practice.

By contrast, Jesus demanded that priority be placed on human pain, suffering, and need. Jesus confronted his critics with the fact that even they recognize that certain emergencies had to be taken care of on the Sabbath: "Suppose one of you, has only one sheep and it falls into a pit on the Sabbath; will you not lay hold of it and lift it out?" (Mt 12:11; Lk 14:6). Then Jesus said, "How much more valuable is a human being than a sheep!" (Mt 12:12). People are of value, ultimate value, in God's eyes. If they suffer, that is a crisis that takes priority over religious tradition and ritual. On holy days one is called by God to save life, not destroy it (Mk 3:4).

Then Jesus grieved because of their hardness of heart said, "Stretch out your hand," and the man's withered hand was restored, healed, re-created. After this the religious authorities held counsel with the priestly politicians as to "how to destroy him" (Mk 3:6; Mt 12:14).

Jesus waged a running battle over God's priorities in life. The religious establishment said ritual and tradition took priority, even if it meant human suffering. Jesus claimed that God gave priority to the alleviation of human suffering. If there were conflicts between tradition and alleviation of suffering through the re-creation of life, Jesus had no doubt as to where God was in the debate. When his disciples were hungry on the Sabbath, their hunger took priority over Sabbath tradition (Mt 12:1-8). When evaluating the weightier matters of the law, mercy and justice took precedence over traditional religious observances (Mt 23:23). Jesus stood within a long prophetic tradition within Israel, in which mercy, righteousness, and justice for people were always prioritized ahead of religious ritual and tradition of any kind. The prophets had brought this word from the Lord:

> "I take no delight in your solemn assemblies. . . . Take away from me the noise of your songs; . . . But let justice roll down like waters, and righteousness like an ever-flowing stream" (Amos 5:21-24; Is 1 and 58; Jer 7).

Jesus was absolutely convinced that for God it was people that counted. God saw their afflictions, heard their cries, knew their suffering, and willed to restore and re-create them. Faithfulness to God would be indicated most clearly in sharing love and service with humanity. To Jesus' enemies, who placed a religious holiness tradition and practice as the top priority in life, Jesus was a dangerous heretic who threatened the authentic faith and life of the Jewish community. A whole way of life was at stake; a whole religious structure that guaranteed the tradition was endangered. The enemies of Jesus decided he had to die! Liberating people from disease and demons made Jesus a major publicity event in first-century Judea. Liberating them from the shackles of traditional religious authoritarianism with its dehumanization of life nailed Jesus to the cross outside the gates of the Holy City.

The Vulnerability of the Messianic Mission

The biblical faith portrays Jesus' life and mission as conflict and combat between the arrival of God's messianic kingdom and the powers of satanic evil. It sees those powers embodied in Jesus and in Jesus' adversaries. Jesus is portrayed in combat: in debate with antagonists, healing the sick and casting out the enemy powers from the possessed, raising life out from the realm of death. However, within this struggle Jesus refused to participate in a violent, revolutionary battle on behalf of political freedom, justice and righteousness. Jesus' prophetic ministry ended in seeming defeat on a cross. Life within God's kingdom is thereby defined as combat not by might but by the spirit of love, which willingly is vulnerable unto death. Jesus certainly awakened hopes of a revolutionary struggle for justice and peace within the crowds and his disciples. John Dominic Crossan in *The Historical Jesus* devotes two excellent chapters to describing the militant, revolutionary context in which Jesus lived.[27]

The New Testament gives only glimpses of this possibility. John reports that after the feeding of the 5,000, Jesus withdrew because he knew that they wished by force to make him king (John 6:15); the Gospels report that one of his disciples, Simon the Zealot, was called from the ranks of the militant revolutionaries (Lk 6:16); the passion narratives report that Peter attempted to defend Jesus with a sword as Jesus was being betrayed by Judas Iscariot. Luke reports a question asked of Jesus by the disciples: "Lord, should we [plural] strike with a sword?" (Lk 22:49). John Howard Yoder believes that the second temptation of Jesus in the wilderness (Luke's order, Lk 4:5-8) was Satan's offer of "all the kingdoms of the world" through military conquest ("if you bow the knee before me").[28]

Within a revolutionary situation with its calls to militant insurrection, Jesus insisted on a nonmilitant struggle. Jesus denounced the rich and powerful, whether Roman or Jewish, for their oppressive and destructive relationships with the poor (Lk 6:20-26); however, Jesus refused to rally the hate and the vengeance of the poor and oppressed. In contrast, Jesus said, "But I say to you that listen, love your enemies, do good to those who hate you, bless those who curse you, pray for those who abuse you" (Lk 6:27-28). Note in particular when Jesus speaks to the Roman laws of occupation, which required Jewish civilians to carry the army pack of Roman soldiers for a mile. "If anyone forces you to go one mile, go also the second mile" (Mt 5:41). It is probable that Jesus' refusal to accept the leadership of a people's revolution on Palm Sunday (Luke 19) is the reason that many of those who welcomed him to Jerusalem also called for his crucifixion and the release of a jailed revolutionary, Barabbas (Lk 23.19).

God limits God's messianic, transforming power within history to insistent and persistent love. That means God's messianic kingdom is vulnerable among us. Divine vulnerability means humanity can always say no to God's call to participate in God's messianic future. God's ultimate intentions can continually be frustrated. Furthermore, it means that God within history has chosen not to call on any authoritarian forces to protect or enforce God's ultimate will within life. God allows God's messianic cause, God's program or project, to be frustrated—even seemingly crushed. Jesus was hung in the terrifying darkness of Holy Friday, and heaven remained in apparent silence. Faith alone had the privilege of witnessing eternity's affirmation of Jesus crucified. Only faith sees the resurrected one and hopes within history's tragedies that the vulnerable God is the God to whom the future of humanity and the cosmos belongs!

The God manifest in Jesus crucified has nothing in common with numerous portraits of God created within our culture. The God of Jesus cannot be identified with the God who blesses the United States or any nation's security or military power. The God of Jesus has nothing in common with any God who promises financial reward, physical comfort, or a life without struggle for God's people. The God of Jesus challenges, critiques, and judges all forms of power and imperialism—cultural, economic, racial, or political. In contrast to the demons and divinities of invincibility worshiped and celebrated by American culture, the God of Jesus is essentially marked by vulnerability, by an infinite capacity to share and bear the cumulative weight of human pain and suffering. This is God concretized in Jesus crucified and risen, the Cosmic Crucified. This is the God who takes the form of outstretched, open, spike-pierced hands, the God who is embodied in a half-naked human figure washing fishermen's feet, the God who like a mother hen scurries about clucking, gathering chicks under her wings in order to absorb the threat of death in her own body, the God who like a mother in childbirth gasps and cries to bring forth a new creation.

One of the most essential things that Jesus' cross says about God is that God does not meet humanity's common expectations. God is the ultimate source of light and life, the ultimate power behind the wind, the waves, and nuclear energy. God is often defined as the omnipotent (all-powerful) and the omniscient (all-knowing). Humanity has normally assumed that when the omnipotent appears, it will be perfectly obvious that God is here. One assumes that evil should crumble and mercy and justice prevail. Millions still argue that Jesus could not possibly be God's Messiah or Anointed Ruler because evil still flourishes.

If Jesus crucified is the Promised of God, then God manifests Godself in paradoxical form. God is revealed as the God who wills not to be "God." God manifests Godself in that which appears to be weakness, foolishness, lowliness. Paul writes, "We proclaim Christ crucified, a stumbling block to Jews and foolishness to Gentiles" (1 Cor 1:23). Christians have also described God as the one who appears to be hidden or concealed among us. In reality God is not hidden, but revealed in Jesus. God appears to be hidden only from the perspective of our expectations. God as the Cosmic Crucified is revealed as the one we did not expect.

Jesus' ministry was marked by the unexpected. Jesus said, "The kingdom of heaven is like treasure hidden in a field" (Mt 13:44), like leaven hidden in three measures of flour (Mt 13:33), like a tiny mustard seed hidden in the ground (Mt 13:31). Even John the Baptist, who had recognized the Messiah's arrival in Jesus (Mt 3:11-17), had serious questions about the nature of Jesus' ministry. It certainly did not appear "God-like" in John's eyes. He had expected more powerful signs and activities of a vice-regent of God (see Mt 3:11-17). John sent messages to Jesus saying, "Are you he who is to come, or shall we look for another?" (Mt 11:3). Jesus replied, "Go and tell John what you hear and see: the blind receive their sight . . . and blessed is he who takes no offense at me" (Mt 11:4-6).

Jesus knew that God's kingdom was present but certainly not obvious. One could stumble if one did not have eyes to see and ears to hear, because God was present in unexpected, surprising, and paradoxical form. God was hidden as the one who chooses not to be "God." Jesus crucified crystallizes and ultimately concretizes that dimension of our faith. If God is the God who allows God's Son to cry into heaven's seeming silence, "My God, my God, why have you forsaken me," then God certainly is hidden in the cross. Martin Luther in the Heidelberg Disputation writes, "For this reason true theology and recognition of God are in the crucified Christ."[29]

However, if it is true that the God who chooses not to be God is truly God, then no hell nor power can separate us from the love of God in Christ Jesus our Lord (Rom 8:38-39). When human experience seems to indicate the absence of God, when suffering and pain are met by the silence of eternity, then either God is not here or God is present but hidden within the suffering of human existence. The gospel of the Cosmic Crucified Jesus claims that God is present, though seemingly hidden, even in the depths of the most tragic suffering and death. The crucified Jesus was raised from the dead. God's promise is that no matter how deep one descends into the hell of human existence, God is still there: There is nothing that can separate us from the [hidden] love of God in Christ Jesus our Lord (Rom 8).

"God lets [God]self be pushed out of the world onto the cross. [God] is present as weak and powerless in the world, and that is precisely the way, the only way, in which [God] is with us and helps us. Matthew 8:17 ("This was to fulfill what had been spoken through the prophet Isaiah, 'He took our infirmities and bore our diseases.'") makes it quite clear that Christ helps us, not by virtue of his omnipotence, but by his weakness and suffering."[30] How does this vision of the vulnerability of God further shape our understanding of the Mission of God?

Jesus Crucified:
Divine Vulnerability Unto Death for the Ungodly

In Jesus, we trust that God through costly love opens God's own being to pain and suffering; that is, to being wounded and vulnerable. In contrast to ancient Greek philosophical views which still influence our theology and in contrast to our culture's glorification of power and domination, the God of the Scriptures is totally involved in human brokenness and suffering as suffering servant. Christians believe that God wills to be open to suffering, to bear suffering in order to save humanity from their own self-destruction. Suffering is not imposed upon a helpless God; rather, God, the Source of cosmic power, wills to be vulnerable to death for the world's sake. The Bible proclaims that God suffers because of us and for our transformation.

A number of Old Testament biblical pictures prefigure this suffering God who became concretized, revealed and identified in Christ: God who as father or mother teaches Israel to walk and embraces them in God's arms and weeps as they walk to their own destruction (Hos 11:1-9); God as a mother in birth pangs gives birth to a new creation (Is 42:14-16); God as husband agonizes with an unfaithful spouse who deserts her husband and family, but then God redeems her and restores her to the home (Hosea 1-3). This prophetic understanding of the suffering love of God is also portrayed in Jesus' parables of the forgiving father who agonizes and then rejoices at his son's return, the shepherd who was anxious and then rejoiced in finding a lost sheep, and the woman who had lost and then found coins (Luke 15). God loves us passionately enough to be moved by us, affected by us, even wounded and pained by us. God suffers, and God is open to being wounded (is vulnerable) because God wills to relate to life and loves people. It is this compassionate and therefore suffering God incarnate in Jesus who is the ground of humanity's redemption. Grace is costly grace!

I remember first reading Kazo Kitamori's book, *The Theology of the Pain of God*, as a seminary student in 1956.[31] Interpreting the Hosea 11:8 passage, "How can I give you up, O Ephraim!", Kitamori spoke of the pain of God. The pain of God is rooted in love that first flows to and encompasses God's people. However, this first love is faced with a people of Israel who ignore, reject and desecrate this first love through faithlessness and disobedience. Faithlessness and disobedience arouse wrathful love in God who is repulsed by sin and desires to purge life of that which is evil and destructive. God's love is pained by sin and evil; however, it refuses to reject or exclude the object of wrath. The love of God, in spite of the pain and in the pain, fully embraces sinful humanity. Love which accepts and forgives is rooted in the pain of God. One of Kitamori's key verses is Jeremiah 31:20:

> Is Ephraim my dear son? Is he the child I delight in? As often as I speak against him, I still remember him. Therefore I am deeply moved for him; I will surely have mercy on him, says the Lord.

Kitamori's insight into the internal suffering of God is helpful in discussions within the Muslim community. Muslims often question Christians as to why God cannot freely forgive sin without requiring the sacrificial death of Jesus. It is helpful to speak of that suffering as in part the internal suffering of God analogous to the internal suffering of parents who love wayward and rebellious children, agonizing over their willful self-destruction, seeking for their repentance and renewal, and joyously welcoming them home in spontaneous but costly forgiveness. It is this suffering love of parents that makes forgiveness possible. This makes it clear that the suffering leading to forgiveness is not external to forgiveness nor haphazardly related to forgiveness, but it is suffering love that makes forgiveness possible. Forgiveness is rooted in love which agonizes over the beloved and is not simply the consequence of a capricious fiat.

The biblical faith, however, roots forgiveness in suffering love, but it does not limit divine suffering to the inner being of God. God's love breaks into history in Jesus in order to seek the wayward and rebellious who intentionally despise and reject the God who seeks them. The depths of God's pain, reflected in the Old Testament and Jesus' teachings is seen, heard and touched in Jesus' messianic mission. Here the pain-filled heart of God becomes embodied in a mission that seeks to save the rebellious and culminates on Golgotha. At Jerusalem's gates Jesus weeps for the city that would reject him and then is hung in the darkness of Golgotha. Here we powerfully and ultimately encounter not only the vulnerability of God's love for those who despised him but God's vulnerability to death for them in his Son who seeks them: that is suffering love as God's infinitely costly saving power (Rom 1:16-17).

God in Jesus Christ is God who through the power of love insistently and persistently seeks and then draws persons to the foot of the cross (John 12:32). Jesus in passionate concern pleads even for those who hung him on Calvary. Jesus tongue-lashed them for their hypocrisy, but he wept for them in their refusal to accept truth and life for the world (Lk 19:41). God's power in Jesus is the power to persevere in a pain-filled mission even unto death. It is the power to forgive in the presence of humanity's continual "no!" It is the power to embrace in pain-filled love those who have refused and despised the best God could offer as God sought them through his own servant.

The unity of God and Jesus as Christ is proclaimed by the resurrection. Robert W. Jenson writes, "Only the resurrection of the dead will verify Yahweh's self-introduction as God."[32] This unity is the foundation for our faith. We proclaim that Jesus' cross is also God's cross. We are compelled to say that the cross is not only Jesus' mission way but God's mission way in the world. Not only is Jesus involved and wounded within history, but God is involved and vulnerable within history. It is not just Jesus who forgives while nails are driven into his hands. God also forgives those who nailed Jesus' hands to a wooden cross.

Particularly when talking with Muslims it is important to make clear that Jesus' mission was God's mission; that God was in Christ reconciling the world to himself (2 Cor 5:18). Some Christians and Muslims particularly note that a traditional doctrine of the atonement makes a distinction between the wrathful justice of God and the mercy of Jesus who dies for the sins of the world.

Instead of maintaining the unity of God in Jesus, the Christian community has often portrayed the crucifixion as a struggle between God and Jesus for the future of sinful humanity. Forgiveness has been portrayed as the consequence of the sacrifice of Jesus, the Son of God, to the justice-demanding God, who demanded a terrifying compensation for sin. It has been concluded by some Muslims that Christians are "polytheists" who worship two different realities—a God of wrath-filled justice and a compassionate Son of God, Jesus. Christian witness within the Muslim community must make it clear that the biblical faith does not view God and Jesus in this antagonistic relationship. Jesus' costly love is God's costly love. Jesus' suffering and pain are God's suffering and pain. The cross of Jesus can never be portrayed as a merciful Jesus appeasing and transforming a wrathful, justice-demanding God. It must always portray the suffering and grieving of God incarnate/concretized in Jesus. In Paul's words, God was in Christ reconciling the world to himself (2 Cor 5:18). "For God so loved the world that he gave his only Son" (John 3:16).

Faith asserts that it is here on this particular hill and in this particular prophet from Nazareth that God absorbed the fanatic and tragic rejection of God's very best, God's own final truth, the Father's own Son (Mk 12:1-12). God accepts into God's own being the costly pain and suffering inflicted on Jesus in order that God's love may encompass or embrace the whole of humanity and all creation. Reconciliation is infinitely costly. Atonement and grace have their roots in the grieving God who struggles to bring life into the midst of death and in the tragic life and crucifixion of Jesus.[33]

Jürgen Moltmann in *The Crucified God* writes insightfully concerning the atonement (at-one-ment) in a section entitled a "Trinitarian Theology of the Cross." Kitamori looks into the inner being of God and sees at-one-ment in God's love overcoming God's own wrath in pain. The Cosmic Crucified concretizes that love in living and dying. Moltmann, in seeking to understand the at-one-ment, plumbs the relation of the Trinitarian Father and Son and focuses upon "the abandonment of Jesus by his God and Father" [p 242].[34] "My God, my God why have you forsaken me?" is reported as the dying words of Jesus by the Gospels of Mark and Matthew (Mk 15:34; Mt 27:46). This theme of abandonment is expressed by the Apostle Paul in Romans 8:31: "He who did not withhold his own Son, but gave him up for all of us, will he not with him also give us everything else?" (see also 2 Cor 5:21; Gal 3:13). Jesus the Son suffers, dying in forsakenness, but, Moltmann insists, the Father who abandons him and delivers him up suffers the death of the Son in the infinite grief of love.[35] It is this unconditioned and boundless love proceeding from the grief of the Father and the dying of the Son that reaches forsaken people with new life.[36]

Moltmann's biblical image portrays God as Father giving over his Son to a vulnerable mission. God takes on and in grief bears humanity's brokenness in order to transform the world. God could not transform humanity by brute irresistible force because in breaking human rebelliousness God would destroy human freedom and therefore humanity itself. Humans would simply be transformed into robots on divine puppet strings. Instead, God sends the Son and God's children in a non-coercive, vulnerable mission of love. That mission is violently rejected in the crucifixion of Jesus; however, God's costly mission perseveres and persuasively draws broken and rebellious persons out of death into life.[37]

God's vulnerable mission can be portrayed from images from the Gospels. Jesus loves, seeks, weeps over and forgives sinners; gives identities as infinitely valuable children to the "nobodies" of society; liberates those enslaved by religious piety and those socially ostracized. Jesus challenges the political and cultural authorities who oppress the marginalized, "sinners," poor and weak. His challenges to the dehumanizing and enslaving powers result in the fury of his enemies and his own death on the cross.

Douglas John Hall writes in similar language:

God meets, takes on, takes into God's *own* being, the burden of our suffering, not by a show of force which could only destroy the sinner with the sin, but by assuming a solidary responsibility for the contradictory and confused admixture that is our life. God incarnate and crucified bears with us and for us the 'weight of sin' that is the root cause of our suffering, and that we cannot assume in our brokenness.[38]

Like Jürgen Moltmann, Douglas John Hall argues powerfully that only the persistent vulnerability of love can transform human lives. If the divine will were suppressive power intent upon the eradication of lovelessness, enmity and other expressions of sin, then suppressive power would necessitate the annihilation of human will and therefore humanity. "There is no sword that can cut away sin without killing the sinner."[39]

In order to explore the ineffectiveness of divine suppressive power to save the sinner, Hall observes that there are human situations in which power is totally ineffective. For example, "Who through power tactics, can eliminate the self-destroying habits of a son or daughter?" Who can force the beloved to return love? However, love, willing to be vulnerable rather than destroy, can persevere in love in spite of rejection, and repudiation and . . . penetrate through them. That quality of love has the possibility of transforming people from within. A son or daughter, loved unconditionally, may experience new life; a lost love may return. The powerful love of God incarnate in the Cosmic Crucified has done precisely this, thereby drawing through persistent persuasion the most recalcitrant sinner unto himself. The Apostle Paul experienced that. "While we still were sinners Christ died for us" (Rom 5:8); therefore, the "love of Christ controls us (RSV) [constrains, urges us on (NRSV)]; because we are convinced that one has died for all . . . And he died for all, so that those who live might live no longer for themselves, but for him who died and was raised for them" (2 Cor 5:14-15).

Human transformation is not grounded in divine, coercive imperial power which crushes opposition to God; rather salvation is derived from divine power willing to love, serve, agonize, and die in order that broken, sinful humanity might have life. "Here is the lamb of God that takes away the sin of the world" (John 1:29); ". . . this is love not that we loved God, but that [God] loved us and sent his Son to be the atoning sacrifice for our sins" (1 John 4:10).

Since Jesus Christ crucified is bedrock for the mission of the church, God's costly and unconditional love, offering forgiveness of sins in Jesus' name, will be at the heart of everything we do and say. God's persevering love in Jesus Christ is also the power and possibility of our own life and mission. God promises that in spite of ourselves we are usable and enables us to participate in the mission of God as disciples of the crucified Jesus.

In Pauline terms, justification, being right with God, is God's gift made possible through the infinite suffering of God and the crucified Jesus. "They are now justified by his grace as a gift, through the redemption that is in Christ Jesus" (Rom 3:24). The privilege and peculiar vocation of the church as Jesus' community of disciples is to share the good news of forgiveness, justification, in Jesus Christ crucified, the good news of the cosmic shepherd who lays down his life for his sheep (John 10).

This understanding of the atonement and justification is the basis of our later contrast between costly grace in the gospel and merciful justice in the Qur'an.

Jesus Crucified:
The Continuing Suffering-with-Us God

Jesus crucified and risen reveals that God is passionately involved with broken people and is, in Jesus, vulnerable unto death for their salvation.

However, the Bible does not say that Jesus' death on the cross was God's original and only participation in human brokenness and suffering. Rather, according to the biblical faith, it is very clear that the suffering of the Cosmic Crucified is rooted in the suffering-with-us God who participated in the suffering of the ancient Hebrew slaves (Ex 3:7-8) and who will continue to participate in human suffering until that day when every tear shall be wiped away and death will be no more. God's suffering love is not tangential to history. It is not immersed in history for a few moments on Golgotha; rather, God's suffering love is immersed in human existence until that future when all tears will pass away (Rev 21:4).

Douglas John Hall writes: "Behind the 'must' of Jesus' passion there is the 'must' of the divine *agape*—and it is visible all the way from Eden!"[40]

First, it is essential to note that Jesus' own suffering in the crucifixion is rooted in and preceded by God's suffering-with-us love concretized in Jesus' life and mission. Jesus' death on Golgotha is preceded by the agonizing cries of Jesus for those who would not listen to God's prophetic word. These cries are rooted in the broken heart of Jesus and of God. "Jerusalem, Jerusalem, the city that kills the prophets and stones those who are sent to it! How often have I desired to gather your children together as a hen gathers her brood under her wings, and you were not willing!" (Lk 13:34). As Jesus approached Jerusalem for the last time, Luke reports:

> As he came near and saw the city, he wept over it, saying, "If you, even you, had only recognized on this day the things that make for peace!" (Lk 19:41).

Jesus suffered with those with whom he lived and suffered because of those with whom he lived long before he was hung on Calvary. The Gospels often state that Jesus looked with compassion on his contemporaries. Compassion literally means to suffer with, to love so deeply that one agonizes with someone. The Greek and Hebrew words lying behind the English translation have similar meanings. "When [Jesus] saw the crowds, he had compassion for them, because they were harassed and helpless, like sheep without a shepherd" (Mt 9:36; Mt 14:14, 15:32, 20:34). In theological terms we confess that God's incarnation in Jesus precedes and is the presupposition of the Cosmic Crucified's vulnerability unto death, the heart of the at-one-ment.

Furthermore, the biblical tradition also reflects glimpses of God's compassion, suffering-with-us love, in the Old Testament. God's suffering-with-us love incarnate in Jesus is preceded by God's compassionate presence among the people of God portrayed in the Old Testament. Terence E. Fretheim has written a remarkable book entitled *The Suffering of God: An Old Testament Perspective*.[41] Fretheim states, "It can reasonably be claimed that the idea of a God who suffered with his people had its roots in the Exodus and in the subsequent reflections on the significance of that event."[42] He notes particularly Exodus 3:7-8 (cf. 2:23-25):

> Then the Lord said, "I have observed the misery of my people who are in Egypt; I have heard their cry on account of their taskmasters; Indeed, I know their sufferings, and I have come down to deliver them from the Egyptians."

Fretheim explains the significance of the verbs, *see, hear, know,* indicating that they, particularly *know,* emerge not only from experience but "intimate experience." "God is depicted here as one who is intimately involved in the suffering of the people."[43]

> God is thus portrayed not as a king dealing with an issue at some distance, nor even as one who sends a subordinate to cope with a problem, nor as one who issues an edict designed to alleviate the suffering. God sees the suffering from the inside; God does not look at it from the outside, as through a window. God is internally related to the suffering of the people. God enters fully into the hurtful situation and makes it his own. Yet, while God suffers with the people, God is not powerless to do anything about it.[44]

A moving passage describing God as weeping for the land of God's people is found in Jeremiah 9:10:

> I will take up [NRSV footnote, Hebrew text] weeping and wailing for the mountains, and a lamentation for the pastures of the wilderness, because they are laid waste so that no one passes through, and the lowing of cattle is not heard; both the birds of the air and the animals have fled and are gone.

In Jeremiah, God in love-wrath is compelled to purge Israel for its own sake; but God is with the suffering Israel and shares the pain of its purging.[45] Another perspective of God's participation in the pain of God's people is found in Isaiah's song of God's vineyard, Israel. God plants a vineyard, God's people, and God carefully watches over God's children, God's pleasant planting. God "expected justice, but saw bloodshed; righteousness, but heard a cry!" (Is 5:7) Once again God creates a people, watches over a people, listens to a people and as a result, knows their bloodshed and cries and participates in them. In compassion, God cries, "Woe to those who cause the bloodshed and the cries." God's wrath is an expression of God's compassionate involvement in people's lives and in God's desire that they share justice and righteousness, that they may have life.

Kosuke Koyama, writing in what he calls a Buddhist culture of tranquility, states that to speak of God's wrath in that context is a scandal. Disciplined monks, like the Buddha, are "free from wrath, the anti-Nirvanic emotion." In contrast, the biblical God is so passionately involved in people's lives (in history) that God shares the pain of injustice and brokenness. It is God's love (*agape*) that loves so deeply that God's righteous wrath wills to purge and transform cultures, nations and peoples.[46]

The biblical tradition sees the suffering-with-us God present and active before the incarnation and Jesus' crucifixion and also continuing after the death and resurrection of Jesus.

This passionate solidarity of God with human suffering continues until the close of the age. This continuing compassion is powerfully portrayed in Jesus' parable of the last judgment in Matthew 25:31-46. In that parable the Son of Man who presides over the judgment says, "I was hungry and you gave me food, I was thirsty and you gave me something to drink. . . . I was a stranger and you did not welcome me, naked and you did not give me clothing . . . as you did or did not do it to one of the least of these, you did not do it to me." Of deepest significance in this parable is the announcement that God in God's agent of judgment is so intimately wrapped up in human existence that God actually experienced the pain of hunger, nakedness, and loneliness as well as being fed, clothed, and comforted with God's children. This passionate solidarity with people will continue "to the close of the age."

Like the Old Testament, the New Testament speaks of God's continuing suffering because of humanity's continuing sin and rebellion. God still grieves when people turn away from God and walk into their self-chosen darkness. Jesus' parable of the prodigal son portrays a father who exuberantly rejoices when a lost son returns home. Joy bursts forth from a father who had agonized with his son in his absence and who "was filled with compassion (suffering-with-us love)" when he saw him approaching from afar (Lk 15:20). The joy and suffering in heaven (God and angels) (Lk 15:10) portrayed in this parable of Jesus describes a God who, until all tears are wiped away, continues to participate in the agony of those who are wayward family and yet beloved. A passage in Ephesians picks up this theme in an exhortation to live within the will of God: "And *do not grieve* the Holy Spirit of God, with which you were marked with a seal for the day of redemption" (Eph 4:30).

In previous paragraphs, references to Israel's brokenness and suffering and to Matthew 25 imply that brokenness, oppression and suffering are physical as well as spiritual and psychological. Psychological, social, and spiritual brokenness and suffering are obviously real, torturous and devastating. The spiritual agony of persons who know that they have betrayed God and themselves, the loneliness of life when sin tears peoples lives apart, the hopelessness that can be experienced when those most loved are suddenly crushed or gone, the meaninglessness of life when purpose disappears—all are experiences of brokenness, inner pain and suffering. The incarnation is God's promise that God participates in that psychological, social and spiritual pain. Hunger, thirst, nakedness, the denial of freedom, imprisonment are also experiences of brokenness and pain. The promise of Jesus crucified is that God has descended into the depths of the sum total of corporate agony. A theology of the cross is rooted in God's passionate, costly involvement in the pain and suffering of cosmic and human life. "The Word became flesh and lived among us . . ." (John 1:14). That in itself is "good news" when all visible signs point to the absence of God or the distance of God.

Christians who are citizens of the U.S.A. and members of an affluent church will perhaps be surprised that much of the two-thirds world will find gospel (good news) in the very announcement that God incarnate in Jesus Christ is present in the midst of the world's poverty and oppression and that God in Christ continues, as in ancient Israel, to hear the cries of God's broken and suffering people. In Jesus' parable of the last judgment (Mt 25:31ff) that is exactly what Jesus promises. It is the promise of the Cosmic Crucified that whenever a child is hungry, Christ shares the hunger; whenever a mother weeps at the death of her child, Christ weeps; whenever a person is maligned or cursed, Christ is maligned and cursed; whenever a human is beaten to death Christ dies again. That in and of itself is gospel when the marks of life within poverty, oppression and death are read to mean the absence or distance of God. C. S. Song movingly writes, "In suffering or in death, namely, in the situation of utter despair and emptiness, we are not alone. We do not suffer alone and die alone."[47]

The mission and message of Jesus needs to be lived out among the world's peoples. The God of Jesus is not the God of U.S. imperial power nor Christian Zionism, but the God who shares their poverty cries and dreams.

In the previous section, "Jesus Crucified: Divine Vulnerability Unto Death for the Ungodly," the historical once-for-allness of Jesus' death was emphasized. In this section, the "continuing suffering-with-us God" has been focused upon. It is possible that someone may interpret this as contradictory; however, it is also possible that the gospel is so rich and has such depth, that two or more affirmations are essential to the Christian witness. The Lutheran tradition of both . . . and (*simul . . . et*) certainly recognizes this. We are both sinners and saints. At the Lord's Table we receive both bread and the body of Christ. It is faithfulness to the biblical tradition that compels one to say both: Christ died once for all, and the Cosmic Crucified continues to suffer with and for his people.

This presentation of a theology of the cross affirms that Jesus was crucified because of and for our sins once for all, and at the same time, through Jesus, we look into the heart of God and find a compassionate God who in love has agonized with the human community from the origins of the human race and will continue to participate in human suffering until that future moment when all tears shall be wiped away. It is therefore not surprising that one sees the marks or footsteps of that costly pain-love of God in Exodus, Hosea, Jeremiah and Isaiah or may even find glimpses of it in Buddhist reflections on the *bodhisattva*, the person who sacrifices *nirvana* in order to continue to share human suffering until others also know the way out of the pain of human existence. Even though this incarnate God is unknown to people, God is already present and active in their lives and desires that the depths of God's saving love in Christ might be known by them.

Trinitarian theology implies that God active within Israel, incarnate in the Cosmic Crucified and as Spirit fills the universe with life and hope, is the same God who created the cosmos; permeates every corner of an expanding 50 billion light-year universe; continually upholds, creates and orders the cosmos; and the same God who at some future point will bring all cosmic history to God's intended fulfillment.[48]

If I were an artist, I would like to paint on a gigantic scale an image that would capture something of the infinity and depth of space and galaxies, broken humanity, and God's saving act of grace in Christ. Concretely on a hill would hang on a cross a lonely, tortured figure whose shadow was cast across a multitude of shattered human faces and stretching out to the boundaries of space and time. It is a trinitarian faith that believes that the cross of the Cosmic Crucified lies within the heart of God and therefore the heart of the universe. A trinitarian faith believes this because the resurrection and the Holy Spirit affirm that God has identified Godself in the crucified Jesus and therefore God has been embodied and revealed in Jesus Christ. Jesus Christ becomes for faith the window through which one looks into the heart of the universe. D. M. Baillie in his book *God Was In Christ* quotes Charles Allen Dinsmore who wrote: "'There was a cross in the heart of God . . . before there was one planted on the green hill outside Jerusalem.'"[49]

This faith announces that Jesus crucified and risen is already present in the world's agony before the gospel is announced. This faith says, "Let me tell you of that one whom you do not yet truly or fully know." It insists on saying with Hindus, Buddhists and Muslims, "May I tell you what is already revealed in Jesus Christ for you. The God to whom you pray and who has heard your prayers goes through hell itself for you and is in your own hell with you." It is this witness which creates faith in order that all may knowingly live in the Messianic Age inaugurated in Jesus as the concretization of the Kingdom of God.

To put all this briefly, the announcement of Good News from the perspective of this statement is not only a divine linguistic event creating faith; it is a divine linguistic event creating faith in a divine cosmic fact and reality present and active before it is announced. It is present and active because creation and salvation concretized in the death of the Cosmic Crucified are cosmic realities that precede the presence and proclamation of the gospel. The embrace of divine suffering love and forgiveness is a reality within which all humanity lives regardless of culture and religion. The revelation embodied in Jesus is a cosmic reality even before it is revealed or announced.

Affirmation of the suffering-with-us God is an affirmation of continuing passionate involvement rather than distance or indifference in regard to God. We will discuss later that the God revealed and known through Jesus, the Cosmic Crucified, is not acceptable to most Muslims with whom we wish to engage. For most Sunni Muslims, suffering is not appropriate to the divine. Kenneth Cragg writes, "Behind this instinctive sense of things theological in the Qur'an and in Islam lies the conviction that there can be no place for suffering in deity. For 'suffering' seems to imply some external source inflicting it... some inferiority that can be 'subject' to restraint."[50] God as Immanuel and Compassion, as suffering-with-us Love even into the incarnation and unto vulnerability to death, is not fitting to divine sovereignty and glory, according to Muslim thought. This is one of the most problematic and difficult discussions that emerges from Christian-Muslim conversations. Conversations on revelation, salvation, and surrender to the will of God (Islam), return again and again to this point. The point may never be surrendered; it marks a striking difference between Christian and Muslim understandings of God. I have always found it striking that Christian scholars of Islam like Kenneth Cragg, Willem Bijlefeld, and Harold Vogelaar become aware of this distinction and that awareness has led them to a deep appreciation of this motif within the gospel message.

Our discussions with Buddhists will take an entirely different path. Buddhists see suffering or impermanence as the essential mark of human existence. That is simply the basic reality of life from which one seeks release. One Buddhist scholar expressed deep appreciation for this missiology of the cross, because it takes human brokenness very seriously; however, he understandably thought that reference to Jesus' as normative was questionable. Another observed that God is irrelevant to the Buddhist quest for release. With Muslims, one discusses the nature of God. With Buddhists, one must begin at a more fundamental level, namely, God.

Chapter 3

Contemporary Challenges
to Christian Witness
and Mission

The Challenge to Arrogance in Witness and Mission

One of the most articulate critics to traditional Christian mission is Wesley Ariarajah, an ordained Methodist minister from Sri Lanka and former Director of the Sub-Unit on Dialogue of the World Council of Churches who now teaches at Drew University. In his publication, *Hindus and Christians: A Century of Protestant Ecumenical Thought*[51] (an excellent work based upon his doctoral dissertation), Ariarajah points to the negative impact that traditional Christian witness has had within the recipient cultures and societies. What makes Ariarajah's discussion extremely significant is the fact that he is an Asian Christian who has always lived and reflected on his Christian faith and ministry within an Asian and primarily a Hindu context.

Ariarajah's concern arises out of an Asian pastoral ministry in which Christian claims to the finality of Christ often led to ministries and witness that were marked by arrogance and intolerance rather than what Kosuke Koyama calls the "crucified mind" of Christ.[52] This experience compels Ariarajah to continually note that Christian affirmations concerning the finality of Jesus Christ have of seeming necessity led to Christian arrogance and intolerance. In the closing chapter of *Hindus and Christians*, he asserts: "Our study of developments within the [Asian] ecumenical movement has shown that every attempt to reflect theologically about other faiths that has begun with the finality of Jesus Christ, interpreted in its various forms, has ended in Christian chauvinism and paternalism."[53]

He concludes that the terms "finality and uniqueness" are obsolete because of the inherent negative implications for Christian relationships and witness among peoples of other faiths.

This conclusion, however, has not led Ariarajah to conclude that Christian witness is illegitimate. It rather has driven him back to the biblical tradition to attempt to discover another approach to religious pluralism. In an earlier publication he wrote: "I am firmly convinced that there is in the Bible another attitude to people of other faiths that Christians in Asia and elsewhere need to recover and celebrate."[54] Ariarajah then lifts up throughout the Bible themes that point to an inclusive rather than exclusive interpretation of the gospel and a path that leads to dialogue rather than confrontation.

Ariarajah begins with the biblical understanding of creation. One God is the creator of everyone, and there is no other provider but this one God. He writes: "People [who are themselves created in the image of God] may or may not have an adequate understanding of who this God is, and their worship may or may not do justice to their understanding of God; but ultimately they are all provided for by this one God. Therefore, from God's side there can only be one family, the human family."[55]

The universal creation theme is followed by universal human alienation from God (the fall) resulting in the universal judgment of the flood. However, it does not stop here, because the Bible goes "on to develop the concept of God's covenant relationship with the whole human family."[56] The universal covenant made with Noah includes more than humanity, because a compassionate God embraces all living things.

The Bible places the story of the chosen Israel in this universal context and sees the election of Israel as a means whereby God will bless all nations through Israel. "I will give you as a light to the nations, that my salvation may reach to the end of the earth" (Is 49:6b). The early Christian community saw this prophetic vision being fulfilled in Jesus Christ and the mission of the body of Christ. "But you are a chosen race, a royal priesthood, a holy nation, God's own people, in order that you may proclaim the mighty acts of him who called you out of darkness into his marvelous light" (1 Pt 2:9). Ariarajah points out that as a consequence of this biblical history, there are two communities of faith (Judaism and Christianity) who identify themselves as instruments of God's light. May it not be possible, argues Ariarajah, that God may also have called and chosen other nations whose divine election lies outside of the scope of the biblical narrative?[57]

Ariarajah states that the Bible itself may give glimpses of a universal activity of God, who in love chooses, calls and judges all nations. Amos, chapters 1 and 2, declares God's particular judgment upon a cluster of Middle East kingdoms, including Damascus, Edom, Moab, Gaza, Tyre, Ammon, as well as Judah and Israel. The Lord roars from Zion because the kingdom of Moab burned to lime the bones of the king of Edom (Amos 2:1). The Lord is passionately concerned about the conduct and the fate of people beyond the covenant with Israel and Judah. Ariarajah states that the prophet goes even further in saying that God has been in the history of these nations because "I brought the Philistines from Crete and the Syrians from Kir, just as I brought you [Israel] from Egypt" (Amos 9:7).[58] God is Lord of history and the nations. This is most powerfully announced in Isaiah 45 when Cyrus, king of Persia, is designated as the Lord's chosen. The Lord has chosen Cyrus to be king. He has appointed him to conquer nations (Is 45:1). A peculiar passage in Isaiah 19 brings to an eschatological climax this prophetic vision of God's relationship to the nations:

> On that day there will be a highway from Egypt to Assyria, and the Assyrians will come into Egypt, and the Egyptians into Assyria, and the Egyptians will worship with the Assyrians. On that day Israel will be the third with Egypt and Assyria, a blessing in the midst of the earth. (Is 19:23-24)

Ariarajah notes that Israel's own prophets insist that the God who called Israel out of Egypt cannot be locked up as Israel's private property. Christian theology, like this biblical tradition, "should allow God to be God."[59]

It is fascinating (but not mentioned by Ariarajah)to read Genesis 21:8ff within the context of this Biblical vision and the context of Christian-Muslim conversations. When Hagar and Ishmael are sent out from the house of Abraham and as they are at the point of dying in the wilderness, God speaks to Hagar:

> "What troubles you, Hagar? Do not be afraid; for God has heard the voice of the boy where he is. Come, lift up the boy and hold him fast with your hand, for I will make a great nation of him." (Gn 21:17b-18)

Ariarajah also sees the Jesus of the Synoptics reflecting this inclusive prophetic theme. Jesus announces the coming reign of God. "Jesus' own life is entirely God-centered, God-dependent and God-ward."[60] Ariarajah could also have noted, but did not, that in Luke, Jesus infuriated his own neighbors, the people of Nazareth, by pointing to the inclusivity of God:

> But the truth is, there were many widows in Israel in the time of Elijah, when the heaven was shut up three years and six months, and there was a severe famine over all the land; yet Elijah was sent to none of them except to a widow at Zarephath in Sidon. There were also many lepers in Israel in the time of the prophet Elisha, and none of them was cleansed except Naaman the Syrian. When they heard this, all in the synagogue were filled with rage (Lk 4:25-28).

Ariarajah's search for the inclusive tradition in Scripture concludes with two encounters: Jonah's call to preach repentance to Nineveh, and Peter's call to preach the gospel to the gentile Cornelius.[61]

In both situations, God had to overcome the exclusive parochial vision of God's spokespersons in order that the inclusive vision of God might be fulfilled. In Jonah's case, God's mercy was extended even to the foreign military terrorists of the seventh century B.C.E. Angry and disgusted with God's grace, Jonah resented God's forgiveness of the repentant Ninevites only to hear:

> "And should I not be concerned about Nineveh, that great city, in which there are more than a hundred and twenty thousand persons who do not know their right hand from their left, and also many animals?" (Jonah 4:11)

In Peter's case, God, through a vision, told a reluctant Peter that God has not created anything clean nor unclean (profane nor sacred), whether it be animals or humanity. Peter's vision of exclusivity is transformed by a divine vision of inclusivity: "I truly understand that God shows no partiality, but in every nation anyone who fears him and does what is right is acceptable to him" (Acts 10:34).

Ariarajah, in a sense, pleads with the Christian community to take note of this often hidden or lost theme that runs through the biblical tradition. From his perspective, it is only by tapping this tradition that Christians can be prevented from encountering peoples of other faiths in arrogance and intolerance. Ariarajah, himself, says that this was his own experience. "It was while preparing for a Bible study on the book of Jonah that I 'saw' the radical nature of its message. My interest in dialogue was kindled, and I came to a new awareness of the theological significance of my neighbors of other faith convictions. For me the Bible has never been the same again!"[62]

It needs to be noted that other Christian theologians have explored and affirmed this inclusive theme within the Bible without negating the normative understanding of Jesus Christ, as is done by Ariarajah. Emil Brunner (Reform), M.M. Thomas (Marthoma), Wolfhart Pannenberg (Lutheran), and Catholic theologians Karl Rahner and Hans Küng have affirmed this inclusive theme while at the same time affirming Jesus Christ's unique role.[63] Braaten, for example, interprets this universal dimension of the faith from an eschatological perspective. The risen Jesus Christ is "the personal event in whom God's final revelation has already occurred."[64] God, however, is at work in other communities of faith. The gospel announces that Jesus Christ is the goal to which God has been leading them all along. "The gospel declares that Christ is the manifestation of the truth of what all things shall become in their fullness."[65] Jesus Christ is universal, the church is not. "The church humbly shows to the other religions that it is also on the way."[66] The full meaning of Christ is explored and articulated as new peoples of new cultures and religions interpret Jesus Christ from their ever new perspectives.

The Challenge of Theological Relativism to Mission

Carl Braaten, in his volume, *No Other Gospel*, fears that recent theological developments that relativize the gospel threaten the very existence of the church and its mission.[67] "Christian theology is today teetering on the brink of suicidal confusion."[68] In contrast, Braaten reaffirms a biblical faith in the finality of Jesus Christ and of the appropriateness of the term "absolute" when applied to the eschatalogical kingdom of God proclaimed and revealed in Jesus.[69] Christianity itself and authentic apostolic mission cease to exist if and when the eschatological finality of Jesus Christ is questioned and denied.[70]

Why is Braaten so deeply concerned? What is the threatening Trojan Horse in our midst? Braaten sees the primary threat articulated clearly in the British theologian John Hick. "Today John Hick is carrying [the] relativistic interpretation of Christianity to an extreme, with uncompromising consistency."[71] John Hick advocates a Copernican revolution in theology, a switch from a traditional Christ-centered (Christocentric) theology to universalistic God-centered (theocentric) theology of religion. Hick argues that our experience of religious pluralism indicates that Jews, Christians, Muslims, Sikhs and Hindus worship an ultimate Being designated by them as Adonai, or God, Allah, Param Atma, Rama, or Krishna. Hick asks, "Do these names designate different gods or are these names for the same ultimate Being?" He suggests three possible answers: 1) there are many gods; 2) one faith-community worships God while the others vainly worship images existing in their imagination; and 3) the most probable is

> that there is one God, who is maker and Lord of all; that in his infinite fullness and richness of being he exceeds all our human attempts to grasp him in thought; and that the devout in the various great world religions are in fact worshipping that one God, but through different, overlapping concepts or mental images of him.[72]

Hick also argues that the Christian doctrine of the incarnation, with its claims to universal finality for Jesus Christ, is an early Christian myth that is no longer tenable in the 20th century.[73] Hick does affirm that Jesus has become for Christians our "sufficient and saving point of contact with God" and therefore there is something absolute about him for our experience, which justifies for us the absolute language which Christianity has developed. If we understand our confession in this way, "We can revere Christ as the one through whom we have found salvation, without having to deny other points of reported saving contact between God and man."[74]

Hick concludes we are picturing a future in which the different religious traditions no longer see themselves as rivals but as mutually enriching communities of faith who have various saving points of contact with God.

Paul Knitter, in his early influential work, *No Other Name?*, concluded his volume with this vision of mutually enriching communities of faith (Knitter designates this approach as "unitive pluralism"):

> Whether Jesus does or does not prove to be final and normative, is not, really the central issue or the primary purpose of dialogue. The task at hand, demanded of Christianity and all religions by both the religious and the socio-political world in which they live, is that the religions speak and listen to each other, that they grow with

and from each other, that they combine efforts for the welfare, the salvation, of humanity.[75] (Please see this endnote.)

It is this relativistic approach to the world of religious pluralism articulated so consistently by John Hick and the early Paul Knitter that Braaten sees as a denial of apostolic faith and as undermining the biblical understanding of the apostolic imperative for mission. In an earlier book, Braaten wrote, "All we know is that we must witness to the truth of Christ in the midst of the world religions, or our faith is dead."[76]

Affirming a Normative "Biblical Tradition"

Hick, Knitter and Ariarajah, as advocates of a Copernican revolution in Christian theology (moving from a christocentric to a theocentric perspective), are thoroughly aware that the New Testament makes numerous exclusive claims concerning Jesus, the Christ. Paul Knitter writes:

> There is another feature of New Testament christology that the previous section did not treat . . . much of what the New Testament says about Jesus is *exclusive*, or at least *normative*. Jesus is the "one mediator" between God and humanity (1 Tim 2:5). There is "no other name" by which persons can be saved (Acts 4:12). Jesus is the "only begotten Son of God" (John 1:14). No one comes to the Father except through him (John 14:6). Just as all died in one man, Adam, so all will be brought to life in one man, Christ (1 Cor 15:21-22). What took place in him was, once and for all (*epaphax*) (Heb 9:12).[77]

Knitter states that this exclusive theme is undeniable. Therefore, the question is raised as to how these exclusive claims are to be interpreted when one no longer accepts them as normative. Both Ariarajah and Knitter see an answer in interpreting exclusive language as confessional language analogous to personal language rooted in relationship and commitment. Both Ariarajah and Knitter use analogies from the personal language of love. Ariarajah writes, "When my daughter tells me that I am the best daddy in the world, and there can be no other father like me, she is speaking the truth. For this comes out of her experience."[78]

Knitter, in a similar vein, asserts, "Exclusivist Christological language is much like the language a husband would use of his wife (or vice versa): 'You are the most beautiful woman in the world' . . . . Such statements in the context of the marital relationship and especially in intimate moments are true."[79] In the realm of personal language, these statements are true; however, in another sense they are not necessarily objectively true statements. It is argued that the exclusive claims for Christ are faith/ confessional statements made by believers whose "love" experience with Christ leads to true, but not absolutely true, statements about their Lord.[80]

Ariarajah writes: "The problem begins when we take these confessions of personal experience and preference and turn them into absolute truths. It becomes much more serious when we turn them into truths on the basis of which we begin to measure the truth or otherwise of other faith-claims."[81] Ariarajah asserts that absolute claims are not possible from a fallible human perspective. Furthermore, when absolute claims of truth are made, intolerance, arrogance and unwarranted condemnation of others immediately arise. This does not mean that Christians will not or should not make their own personal faith statements concerning their personal or communal convictions and commitments arising from their encounter with God in Jesus Christ. However, such statements, concerning God are to be seen within the context of other faithful persons and faith communities who have looked for God's universal revelation through other windows of faith.

It is at this point that we may ask whether the theological position of Ariarajah and Knitter is adequate or "absolutely true." Are there not questions that need to be raised? **For example, does one absolutely trust that which is not believed to be authentically true, and therefore normative?** We will continue to affirm that our personal faith language concerning Jesus crucified is not only language of personal preference but normative. We trust that the love concretized in Jesus is the Cosmic Reality in whom all peoples of all nations may ultimately trust. Our own theological language may be questioned as historically relative; however, through that language, we will continue to affirm that the life-affirming and transforming, all-embracing, vulnerable and suffering love concretized in Jesus is normative, the ultimate Cosmic Reality which can be "trusted" even when stars disintegrate. For us that conviction is grounded in the love God embodied in Jesus which grasps us, and in Jesus being raised by the Spirit which is a living reality in our lives. We trust that it is God who spoke in Jesus and has raised Jesus. In so doing God announces that historical relativity has been transcended in the love concretized in the Cosmic Crucified.

That love concretized in Jesus, however, is not limited to the historical presence of Jesus or a proclamation of Jesus as risen Lord or Son of God. Cosmic love concretized in crucified love is that which ultimately permeates and embraces creation. Our historical engagement with Jesus has made possible trust that lives in acceptance, forgiveness, life-giving Spirit and the victory over fear in the presence of death. We trust that God is not and never will be other than cosmic love identified in crucified love. Within that life-transforming reality we trust that all creation and humanity are embraced. We anticipate meeting that love within all humanity in all of its ethnic, cultural and religious diversity. We further anticipate that cosmic love, concretized in crucified love, will be perverted and distorted in every person, culture, society and religion. We are totally aware that judgment must begin with ourselves. For example, crucified love embodied in Jesus is totally distorted in much of contemporary American Christianity where the U.S. imperial empire and values supersedes the Jesus movement.

When Christian's claim Truth it is the truth of cosmic love concretized in crucified truth. In the words of the Gospel of John 1.14, Justin Martyr (The Apology I.46), Clement (The Stromata Book I, Chapters 4-5) and Augustine (The Retroactions Chapter 12), the Logos (Cosmic Love which permeates all creation) became flesh (crucified love). Such love transcends historical relativity.

Capturing the Heart of the Mission of Jesus

Having asserted the historical relativity of the gospel, Ariarajah then moves on to claim that dialogue, openness to people of other faiths, and mutual enrichment through shared life and conversations flow from the heart of the Bible. This central message is the good news concerning God's love, the nature of God's love, and what that love meant in terms of God's relationship to the world.

Christians speak of this love as a consequence of meeting God in Jesus' life and ministry. Christians "were convinced that, meeting [Jesus], they came into a living encounter with God"[82] and God, seen through Jesus, is a loving God who leads persons into relationships, into dialogue. Ararajah draws this conclusion from the nature of God's love revealed in Jesus' life and mission.

God's love revealed in Jesus is first of all unconditional and prevenient. Jesus' love extends to persons before any positive response is present. God makes the sun to shine and the rain to fall on evil as well as good people, on Jesus' mother's garden as well as the vineyards of Herod the King (Mt 5:45). Jesus ate and drank with outcasts and sinners before there were signs of repentance. Significantly, Jesus had time for children even when they were considered a waste of time for his disciples. Ariarajah writes:

> Here the biblical message is unambiguously dialogical. For it insists on the "previousness" of grace, and of God's acceptance of us before our acceptance of God. The people we meet, of whatever religion, race or age, are all in that sense people of God. It is this belief that the other person is as much a child of God as I am that should form the basis of our relationship with our neighbors. That attitude is at the heart of being in dialogue.[83]

Furthermore, Ariarajah states that dialogue is at the very heart of the cross; for the cross, if nothing else, stands for the vulnerability of love. God in Jesus would accept the rejection by humanity before rejecting humanity. God's love in Jesus' cross wills to be self-giving, available, vulnerable, prevenient and unconditional. The incarnation, in this sense, is God's dialogue with the world; "it is an expression of how God always stands [in love] with the human community."[84] Christian mission in response to God's love revealed in Jesus will be molded by this love of God. Ariarajah writes:

> Religious pluralism, let me repeat, does not demand that people give up or hide the witness they have to offer. But it certainly demands that such witness is given in the spirit of one who has truly experienced the humility, the vulnerability and the self-giving that are at the center of Christ's own witness. Such a witness can only be given in the context of a larger vision of the mission of God in which we are partners and fellow pilgrims with all others who also stand within the grace and love of God.[85]

Ariarajah has powerfully argued that self-giving and vulnerable love are central to the Christian vision and authentic Christian witness must be molded by the mind of Christ. He is deeply concerned about this, because he has experienced the devastating consequences created by Christian arrogance and intolerance among Asian peoples. It is this concern that is of primary importance for those who seek to witness to Jesus the Christ within the world of religious pluralism. We believe, however, that Ariarajah's own concern and position imply that the love of God of which he speaks is not simply personal preference but true, authentic and normative for all historical times and places. We are convinced that crucified Truth is God's gift in which all humanity may trust. In the words of Paul, "Every tongue will confess that Jesus is Lord" (Phil 2:11). Truth is crucified Truth.

Ariarajah's concern is reiterated by many voices from around the globe. When Professor Kosuke Koyama met with the American Lutheran Church/Division for World Mission and Inter-Church Cooperation task force assigned to explore Christian witness among Buddhist peoples, he stated emphatically that Western Christians should not and could not address an engagement of Christians and Buddhists in Asia unless they first confessed that the stance of many countries, organizations, churches and missionaries in Asia had been a stance of arrogance, paternalism and oppressive control. In contrast, Koyama calls all Christian missionaries out from a crusading mind-set to a crucified mind, the mind of Jesus Christ (Phil 2:5-11).[86]

A few years ago, Dr. Harold Vogelaar and I had the privilege of talking with the director of the Muslim Mission to the World. In the midst of the conversation, the director said, "How can there be genuine engagement between Muslims and Christians while Christian nations systematically destroy our Palestinian brothers on the Gaza strip?" As a Muslim, he saw the betrayal of the Palestinian people after World War I, when political independence had been promised and denied, and after World War II, when the traditional homeland of the Palestinian people had been given to Jewish immigrants, as a breach of human trust that made Christian and Muslim relationships tenuous at best. Muslim peoples had been subjugated to the military and political terror of the arrogant and imperialistic West.

The question is raised from around the globe as to the possibility of separating a Western missionary witness to Jesus crucified from the dominating global power of our Western nations. That question is a primary question for the Western Christian community today. In many discussions I have found that some representatives of the Western Christian church find it difficult to take this question seriously. That has not been true in conversations with Christian partners from Latin America, Africa and Asia.

Affirming Cosmic Finality with the Vulnerability of Cosmic Love:

The usefulness of the word "finality" may be questioned by some because it may intimate that God's saving and revealing work is limited to and ceases with Jesus. For others, it may imply Christian imperialism, which is specifically denied here. I have chosen to maintain the word to make clear that the thesis of this document affirms the normativeness and unsurpassability of what happens and is revealed in Jesus crucified. Everything we say and do is grounded in our conviction that Jesus concretizes the reign of God's Love and the words and lives of the Jesus people are to be normed and conformed to Jesus crucified. God's self-identifying, self-characterizing action happens in Jesus crucified and risen. Jesus as the concretized Word of God becomes a normative and unsurpassable revelation of God. God is and will never be other than that. Jesus people are never called to be conformed to other than that.

Having said this, how do we address those who experience and who claim that this "exclusive" position inevitably leads to Christian arrogance and intolerance, which leads to human suffering, alienation and oppression? How do we affirm with Dr. Ariarajah that this is contrary to the mission of Jesus and the revelation of God through Jesus marked by self-giving, humility, openness and vulnerability? How do we do that without giving up our convictions that Jesus as Christ is not only cosmic truth but normative and final cosmic truth?

The Christian community is called to do that by affirming that the risen Christ is precisely the crucified Jesus. The one with nail-pierced hands sits at the right hand of God. In affirming that the crucified is the one who transcends historical relativity, one makes normative the life-affirming, self-giving, serving, sacrificial vulnerable love of Jesus crucified. One makes normative the one who dies to all personal limited visions in order to be raised into the cosmic vision of the Abba and Spirit who called and empowered Jesus as crucified Truth.

It is precisely in exploring the dimensions of Jesus as the crucified one that one discovers the shape of the gospel that has the power to speak authentically among Muslims and Buddhists. Furthermore, it is within this witness and these conversations that we are driven back to Jesus because one finds something wondrously unique about the crucified truth. Where else does one encounter God portrayed as costly love entering so deeply, fully and sacrificially into human existence on humanity's behalf? On a cosmic scale nothing greater can be conceived than that. If we find ourselves skeptical of the reality of that vision, if we wonder whether, in Buddhist terms, it may be an illusion, then one continues to hope that it could be or would be true. That, in and of itself, is an invitation to follow Jesus—to come and see a crucified Jewish prophet who Christians have believed embodies the Kingdom of God![87]

Chapter 4

Jesus' Call to Discipleship: The Way of the Cross

The Christian community is brought into existence by God embodied in Jesus as Christ. It is God, that one who creates and permeates a universe of billions of galaxies, that one who in poetic terms throws stars across the heavens, who incredibly and passionately enters human existence and serves, suffers, agonizes, and is vulnerable unto death. That costly love is the forgiveness of our sins and the possibility of our life in communion with God. God in the Jesus crucified also entered into combat here on behalf of new messianic life in the arriving kingdom of God. The lost/damned are found; the poor are given hope; the sick are healed; the rich, powerful and religiously complacent are challenged. This messianic combat is waged with the power of vulnerable love, seemingly defeated but ultimately victorious as the crucified is raised and sits at the right hand of God. Sin, Satan and death are conquered. The crucified is Christus Victor. God in Christ struggles for life, suffers unto death, and is raised that the cosmos might have life. That is the heart of our mission message.

Because this is the heart of it all, there is often a hesitancy within the Christian community to affirm that the church as the body of Christ in mission is also called to participate in God's struggle and God's suffering love, as well as participating in Christ's gifts of forgiveness and resurrection. That, however, is a reality that permeates the biblical witness. A mark of the church is that while it lives within the victory over sin, death and the devil, it is called to costly mission discipleship to be a serving, sacrificing, suffering church in order that the gospel of the Cosmic Crucified might as light, leaven and salt permeate every dimension of human life and history. This chapter explores the significance of this missiology of the cross for the life-style of the bearer of the gospel who proclaims the lordship of the crucified Jesus. The chapter begins by describing Christian discipleship in mission as being conformed to the Cosmic Crucified. Both the New Testament and Luther speak of the necessity, the legitimacy, relevance and power of a missioning form of life that is conformed to Christ.

This chapter explores discipleship as conformity with God incarnate in Christ in the light of the three dimensions of the cross of Christ described in a previous chapter. This missiology of the cross makes it impossible for the Christian community to separate the mission message from mission deeds. The question is not debatable, as it was not in Jesus' message and in his life! Discipleship in mission is:

1. Discipleship in mission as God's call to passionate involvement in human brokenness and suffering.

2. Discipleship in mission as God's call to participate in the messianic struggle for life in the midst of death.

3. Discipleship as God's call to vulnerability in mission.

Discipleship in Mission as Conformity with Jesus Crucified

One of the most powerful ways that the New Testament speaks of Jesus' call to missioning discipleship is to call the Christian community to conformity with the being and mission of God as it is incarnate in the being and the mission of the Jesus crucified. Walter Altmann writes, "We are free from the necessity to imitate Christ [the impossibility of Christian perfectionism] because his work is fundamental, unrepeatable and complete. But for the same reason we are free [from concern to establish our relationship to God] for new liberating actions [participation in messianic kingdom activities], in *conformation with the cross of Christ* and in accordance with what our imagination and discernment show us to be works of love" (emphasis added).[88]

Discipleship in mission is life in conformation with Jesus crucified. Jesus calls his disciples to take up their cross and follow him (Mk 8:35ff). Jesus promises that the disciples as bearers of the Good News to all nations (Mk 13:10) will be hated and persecuted because of bearing Jesus' name (Mk 13:9-13). Furthermore, in persecution they are blessed by God. "Rejoice and be glad, for your reward is great in heaven, for in the same way they persecuted the prophets who were before you" (Mt 5:11-12).

In Philippians, Paul asserts that he desires, within the mission of the body of Christ, to share in Christ's sufferings (Phil 3:10ff). In

2 Corinthians he writes: "For while we live, we are always being given up to death for Jesus' sake, so that the life of Jesus may be made visible in our mortal flesh" (2 Cor 4:11). In sharing in Christ's sufferings, Paul believes that "I am completing what is lacking in Christ's afflictions [the continuing suffering-with-us God] for the sake of his body, that is, the church" (Col 1:24). Paul states that participation in the suffering of Christ is an introduction to being glorified with Christ (Rom 8:17). Similar themes are found in 1 Peter 2:18-25 and 2 Timothy 2:12-13. In addressing a persecuted and suffering church, Peter wrote, "For to this you have been called, because Christ also suffered for you, leaving you an example, so that you should follow in his steps" (1 Pt 2:21). Conformity with the Cosmic Crucified is costly suffering discipleship that is blessed by God and the privileged possibility of present joy and future glory.

The biblical witness broadens "conformity with the cross" to the whole life of Jesus beginning with the cosmic Christ's condescension in the incarnation and including Christ's forgiving, self-giving love and humble servanthood. Paul calls the Philippian Christians to be conformed to the mind of Christ:

> Let the same mind be in you that was in Christ Jesus, who though he was in the form of God, did not regard equality with God as something to be exploited, but emptied himself, taking the form of a slave...and became obedient to the point of death—even death on a cross (Phil 2:5-11).

The life and mission of the body of Christ is called to a discipleship conformed to this God-formed and cruciform ministry of humble servant-hood that participates in God's vulnerability even to death.

The biblical tradition is rich in servant images, calling and mandating mission in conformity with the Cosmic Crucified. In John, Jesus says, "So if I, your Lord and Teacher, have washed your feet, you also ought to wash one another's feet" (John 13:14). Paul, in calling for generosity for the saints in Jerusalem asserts, "For you know the generous act of our Lord Jesus Christ, that though he was rich, yet for your sakes he became poor, so that by his poverty you might become rich" (2 Cor 8:9). In Galatians, Paul writes, "Bear one another's burdens, and in this way you will fulfill the law [the way] of Christ" (Gal 6:2).

All of these calls to be conformed to the Cosmic Crucified are ultimately calls to be conformed to the love of God revealed and incarnate in Jesus Christ. Love one another as I have loved you (John

13:34, 15:12). "We know love by this, that he laid down his life for us—and we ought to lay down our lives for one another" (1 John 3:16, 4:7-10). This love conformed to Jesus Christ forgives unconditionally (Col 3:13) and loves indiscriminately as God does—even unto the enemy (Mt 5:43-48; Lk 6:32-36). John Howard Yoder in *The Politics of Jesus* has provided an excellent discussion of Christian discipleship as being conformed to Christ in a chapter entitled "The Disciple of Christ and the Way of Jesus."[89]

As noted earlier, Altmann believes that the Lutheran tradition has forgotten "the necessity of following Jesus Christ in his path, of joining Jesus Christ in his *kenosis*, his emptying out."[90] Many Lutherans are often concerned that calls to discipleship might be just one more sinful human attempt to justify oneself in the presence of God. This is particularly true if discipleship is understood as a form of humanly attainable sanctification—a process whereby one makes progress in a life of holiness.[91]

Discipleship, as God's call to conformity to Jesus Christ, has nothing to do with "attaining sanctification" or "self-justification." It is discipleship that experiences being overwhelmed by the awesomeness of God's self-giving, unconditional, costly love, that hears with joy Christ's promise of forgiveness, and rejoices in the privilege that the Cosmic Crucified makes possible in the call, "Come, follow me!"

Authentic discipleship recognizes that there is a tragic gap between the call to conformity with Jesus Christ as God's kingdom way in the world and one's own stumbling efforts to follow in the way of Christ. Therefore, Paul's declaration in Romans 6:1-4 that in Baptism we have died to sin is recognized by Luther in the Small Catechism as a daily drowning of the "old" sinful person in order that the "new" person conformed to Jesus Christ might daily arise to "walk in newness of life."

Question: What does such baptizing with water signify?

Answer: It signifies that the old Adam in us, together with all sins and evil lusts, should be drowned by daily sorrow and repentance and be put to death, and that the new man should come forth daily and rise up, cleansed and righteous, to live forever in God's presence.[92]

Martin Luther's famous document *The Freedom of a Christian* spells out the relationship between gospel and cruciform discipleship in two seeming paradoxical propositions:

1. A Christian is a perfectly free lord of all, subject to none.

2. A Christian is a perfectly dutiful servant of all, subject to all.

Under the first proposition, Luther states that ultimately and solely the Christian's life and future with God is an absolute unconditional gift of God in Jesus Christ. "One thing, and only one thing, is necessary for Christian life, righteousness, and freedom. That one thing is the most holy Word of God, the gospel of Christ."[93] Good works cannot contribute anything to this gift, but, on the contrary, they may be injurious if the Christian believes that one is justified by them.[94]

Luther then turns to the second proposition that the Christian is a "perfectly dutiful servant of all, subject to all." That is conformity to the servanthood of Christ. Luther can even speak of being Christ to the neighbor.

In describing this servanthood, Luther recognizes a continual struggle between the old and the new. The new person in Christ is obedient to God "out of spontaneous love in obedience to God and considers nothing except the approval of God, whom he would most scrupulously obey in all things."[95] However, this new person must struggle with the old within, which is not necessarily willing to die. Therefore, there is the daily dying and rising to be in conformity with the Cosmic Crucified. "So the Christian who is consecrated by his faith does good works, but the works do not make him holier or more Christian, for that is the work of faith alone [trusting receptivity to God's unconditional costly grace]."[96] It is this faith which is active in love (Gal 5:6) and is called to conformity with Christ's servanthood. Luther writes in *The Freedom of the Christian*:

> Although the Christian is thus free from all works, he ought in this liberty to empty himself, take upon himself the form of a servant, be made in the likeness of men, be found in human form, and to serve, help, and in every way deal with his neighbor as he sees that God through Christ has dealt and still deals with him. This he should do freely, having regard for nothing but divine approval.[97]

> Hence, as our heavenly Father has in Christ freely come to our aid, we also ought freely to help our neighbor through our body and its works, and each one should become as it were a Christ to the other that we may be Christs to one another and Christ may be the same in all, that is, that we may be truly Christians.[98]

Gerhard Forde, writing in *Christian Dogmatics*, concludes his discussion of the Christian life with these striking words:

> The Christian vision leads into the world, to suffering for and with others in the expectation of God's will being done on earth as it is in heaven. The aim is not to gain one's own holiness or to bring in the kingdom by force or tyranny, but to care for God's creatures and God's creation. "The creation waits with eager longing for the revealing of the sons of God" (Rom 8:19).[99]

One of the most powerful statements about cruciform life and mission is found in Dietrich Bonhoeffer's *Letters and Papers From Prison*:

> To be a Christian does not mean to be religious in a particular way, to cultivate some particular form of asceticism (as a sinner, penitent or a saint), but to be a man. It is not some religious act which makes a Christian what he is, but participation in the suffering of God in the life of the world.[100]

The biblical tradition as well as the Luther tradition, compels us to rethink both: 1) the cruciform nature of the gospel of the Cosmic Crucified; and 2) the cruciform nature of the ministry of those participating in the mission of God incarnate in the Cosmic Crucified. One must ask in the words of Walter Altmann why the Lutheran church in particular has forgotten "the necessity of following Jesus Christ in his path, of joining Jesus Christ in his *kenosis*, his emptying out."[101]

In the following sections, several implications for "missionary discipleship conformed to the Cosmic Crucified" are outlined. Each section on discipleship in mission relates to a previous section describing the mission of God incarnate in the Cosmic Crucified.

Discipleship in Mission and God's Call to Passionate Involvement in Human Suffering

The continuing suffering-with-us-God incarnate in Jesus has radical implications for the church's mission (see chapter 2). If solidarity with human brokenness and pain defines one dimension of God's mission, then being conformed to Jesus Christ and participation in the mission of God will mean sharing in the brokenness and pain of the human community. In the thoughts of Matthew 25 and Exodus 3, there are afflictions to be seen, cries to be heard, and sufferings to be known. Discipleship is being captured by God in Jesus Christ, who moves into our lives, turning us inside out and upside down in order that we might with the Cosmic Crucified be swept into the world to share the depths of human pain and brokenness. "As the Father has sent me, so I send you" (John 20:21).

The mission of the body of Christ is marked by participation in human lives rather than indifference to and distance from human lives. Participation rather than indifference and distance is to mark every dimension of the life and mission of discipleship. In recent years, Christian ministry in the U.S.A. has been marked by a deep concern for counseling. Prophetic spokespersons in the field of pastoral counseling have called the church into the depths of human suffering. Behind the masks of social convention human lives are lived out in isolation, irresponsibility, guilt and failure as well as other forms of pain. If the mission of the body of Christ is to be conformed to Jesus Christ, it will follow Jesus into the inner depths of human existence. Within every human life there are afflictions to be seen, cries to be heard and suffering to be known. Good parents know this in their children; caring spouses know it in their loved ones and disciples of Christ are called to know it in each other and in the lives of those met in the world. The suffering-with-us God calls the Christian community into the depths of human lives—to be a suffering-with-us people.

The world is marked not only by inner pain but also incredible physical suffering, both corporate and individual. Statistics are so overwhelming that they become seemingly irrelevant to our daily lives. Eight hundred million persons malnourished; 30,000 children dying daily from inadequate diets and health care; 16 million refugees, 13 million orphans on the continent of Africa as a result of the AIDS epidemic; and over 2 billion people in the world without adequate water. Millions of those people live within Muslim and Buddhist communities. Thirteen countries with Muslim majorities of over 75% (seven with majorities over 90%) and with a total population of 500 million people have an average annual per capita income of less than $500 (1990 *Encyclopedia Britannica*). The lives of most of those millions are lived out beyond the horizons of our consciousness. However, Christ shatters the parochialism of our lives and calls us into solidarity with the world's suffering. There are afflictions to be seen, cries to be heard and suffering to be known.

Authentic Christian witness to the good news of the Cosmic Crucified takes place as disciples participate in the pain of the world. Within the pain (in contrast to distance) and in solidarity with suffering (in contrast to indifference) the Christian community proclaims in word and deed the saving power of the gospel. The community, as noted by Walter Altmann, has often neglected the call of God to the cruciform mission of the body of Christ. We often have not heard the radical call to discipleship, to follow Jesus into the depths of human existence.

Discipleship in Mission and God's Call to Participate in the Messianic Struggle for Life in the Midst of Death

The messianic cosmic struggle still permeates human life and history. The coming kingdom of God inaugurated in Jesus and for which we continue to pray ("Your kingdom come; your will be done on earth as in heaven") continues to be engaged in struggle with the demonic powers of darkness. As in Jesus' day, religious traditions dead to the living God continue to enslave human lives; the poor and oppressed continue to be exploited by the world's rich and powerful; the weak and diseased, like Lazarus at the rich man's door, are often neglected and relegated to the periphery of life, where their presence will not disturb.

Contemporary mission discipleship is openness to God's call to participation in the continuing messianic mission of the body of Christ. The powers of darkness are to be met, combat to be entered, demons overcome, battles lost and battles won. The cross indicates that more often than not compassion, self-giving love, and the vulnerability of servanthood will be dominated and even crushed by the powers of evil and destruction. However, the resurrection of the Cosmic Crucified is God's promise to the disciples of Jesus that ultimately the future belongs to the Abba of Jesus. This hope, which transcends both optimism and pessimism, is the driving power of the mission of the body of Christ.

> But thanks be to God, who gives us the victory through our Lord Jesus Christ. Therefore my beloved, be steadfast, immovable, always excelling in the work of the Lord, because you know that in the Lord your labor is not in vain (1 Cor 15:57-58).

The Continuing Prophetic Voice

Discipleship within the messianic struggle is marked by the continuing prophetic voice of the body of Christ. It is the Spirit-empowered voice (Rom 12:6, 1 Cor 12:10) that witnesses to Jesus Christ (Mk 13:11, Acts 1:8) and in Jesus' name challenges the values and norms; that is, the principalities and powers of the twenty-first century. It is this prophetic voice in words and actions that makes the body of Christ the salt and light of the world. In Jesus' words, if this prophetic voice, which speaks an alien word in the world, loses its saltiness, then it has lost its value (Mt 5:13). Likewise, an alien word of light in a world of darkness must be lifted up to give light to the whole house (Mt 5:14). The Cosmic Crucified continually challenges the body of Christ to be about its alien prophetic mission, challenging the powers of darkness.[102]

In the last century, Søren Kierkegaard, the Danish religious thinker, made a devastating attack upon the church of Denmark because of its inability to speak God's alien word of truth within Christendom, which had lost God's truth and lived in its own darkness. Kierkegaard charged that the church had lost its prophetic voice because they had lost their conformity with the prophetic crucified Christ, who had spoken God's prophetic alien truth and suffered death for it.

According to Kierkegaard, the Christ who said, "Follow me," was the Christ in his humiliation, not the Christ in his glory. Thus, the Christian must become contemporary with the Christ who was despised and hated for speaking God's alien prophetic truth. Only after sharing in the humiliation and suffering of Christ can the Christian share in his exaltation.[103]

Wherever people and messianic life are crushed, wherever love is absent, justice perverted, the good betrayed, religion distorted, and the beautiful disgraced, there the alien prophetic voice of the Cosmic Crucified must be enabled to speak. God's prophetic alien word must be heard, Repent, for the kingdom of God is at hand. People are to be challenged to repentance in Jesus' name. For the sake of their own life and for the sake of the lives they ignore and destroy, they are called to repentance and participation in the messianic kingdom. To those who repent, who allow their lives to be turned around and upside down, the Cosmic Crucified promises your sins are forgiven; go in peace. To the recipients of that costly gift, the Cosmic Crucified says, take up your cross and follow me, as aliens in a foreign land.

The Contemporary Damned and Marginalized

Every generation and century has its particular marginalized who are consigned to live outside the circle of the chosen and righteous. In Jesus' day, there were "sinners" whose lives were not lived in conformity with what Marcus Borg terms the politics of holiness. There were also other marginalized: the poor, the oppressed, women, and gentiles, whom Jesus, challenging his contemporaries, incorporated within the circle of the compassion of God.

Mission conformed to Jesus Christ continues to mean crossing boundaries that exclude in order that all may fully participate in the new creation of the inaugurated messianic reign. Those boundaries vary from one culture or nation to another. In India there are the Dalits who are consigned to live outside of the Hindu caste system; in Japan there are the Burakamin who traditionally carried out the "unclean" work of society; in Latin America there are the landless farmers who have been driven from the source of their existence; in the U.S.A., Europe and South Africa, there are racial groups whose skin color denies them full participation in the cultural and economic privileges of society. Within the world of contemporary U.S. politics there is the boundary of hate between straight and gay. The list of marginalized local and global peoples is endless and presents the followers of Jesus with continual challenges to follow the Cosmic Crucified across all boundaries with the self-giving inclusive vulnerability of the mind of Christ.

One of the most critical and universal boundaries of the 21st century is the boundary between male and female. The Christian church confronts this boundary on every continent both in the world and in the church itself, as well as in Muslim, Buddhist, Hindu and other religious communities.

Human culture for thousands of years and yet today exploits women and limits the potential of women in participating within the mission of the body of Christ. It is tragic that a number of persons within our Christian tradition have not been faithful to Jesus Christ, who radically challenged the sexism of his day by teaching women, touching "unclean women," sharing with women companions who later stood faithfully at the cross, and making Mary the first witness to the resurrection. The early church molded by the ministry of Jesus was a radically new community in which there was not Jew nor Greek, free nor slave, male nor female.[104]

Discipleship to Jesus compels us into solidarity with women. One dimension of this solidarity is sensitivity to our God language. Sensitivity to God language is important in tapping the tremendous gifts of women for the mission of Christ. As long as male language is the primary way of speaking of God, people will (and do) conclude that feminine descriptions of God are not appropriate or less adequate in addressing or describing God. This in turn will imply for many that male humans are superior to female humans, having more gifts and potential as participants in the life and mission of the body of Christ. From my own reading, personal counseling and conversations with both women and men, I know this to be true for countless women. I know many women who, like many persons of color, struggle to remain within the church in spite of the fact that the church's male and white cultural language for God, the male chauvinism of many clergy, and the male prejudices prevalent within the Christian and missionary community make that almost intolerable.

In order to affirm that all women in the church are full participants, I believe the church should be sensitive in its use of God language and it should be supporting women as they search the Scriptures for feminine descriptions of God (there are many).[105] Balancing our God language affirms the God-given value of women and empowers the church for witness in the world.

There is another and even more important reason for the use of feminine symbols for God in our particular culture so often marked by domination, arrogance, aggressiveness, militarism and violence. Those characteristics which mark our culture and even our churches and theological discussions are very often designated as male characteristics. Therefore, in our culture to say "God he" implicitly portrays to many people and particularly women a God who is aggressive and domineering if not militant and violent. In contrast, a missiology of the cross states that God is ultimately known in Jesus the Cosmic Crucified, in self-giving love, sacrificial service and vulnerability. These characteristics in our culture are often designated as female. Therefore, "God she" is needed in our culture to speak God's alien word of truth and to witness to God who is incarnate in Jesus and vulnerable to death. I believe that this may be what is most frightening, particularly to males in our church who may be more deeply formed by our culture than cruciformed by the Cosmic Crucified. This male domination is presently increasing in much of the church in opposition to the growing role of women in church and society. Evangelical Fundamentalists demand that women are subordinate to men who are like umbrellas, protecting the family. Mormons, Catholics, Orthodox and other churches still insist that women follow their male compatriots through life.

Struggling with this issue as disciples of Jesus may be one of the most important things we do as we engage with Muslims and

Buddhists around the globe. It is the Cosmic Crucified who compels the Christian community of disciples to see beyond the present destructive cultural walls and boundaries between male and female and to envision a new creation in which there is neither male nor female. Such a vision challenges not only Christians but Muslims, Buddhists, and the world.

The Messianic Mission: The Restoration of the Totality of Creation

Jesus' prophetic, messianic mission was rooted in Israel's faith in God, who created the cosmos and called Israel into a mission of transformation. God is the creator of the heavens and the earth. All of life is God's creative handiwork and is under God's providential care. Jesus saw lilies of the field clothed beautifully and birds of the air fed bountifully by the hands of God (Mt 6:25ff). This same God was at work in Israel's history and spoke through prophetic voices. As promised by the prophets, God was now doing a new thing within creation. God's kingdom/reign was approaching, and all that had been distorted and destroyed by human indifference and disobedience to God would be reclaimed and restored. Jesus sent a message to John saying that the promises of God's new creation envisioned by Isaiah (Is 29:18-19; 35:5-6; 61:1) were being fulfilled:

> The blind receive their sight, the lame walk, the lepers are cleansed, the deaf hear, the dead are raised and the poor have good news brought to them (Mt 11:5; Lk 7:22).

Biblical thought does not dichotomize life between the physical and spiritual in terms of matter and mind. Rather, life is unified by the creative Word and Spirit of God. God speaks and the cosmos exists (Gen 1). God breathes and matter lives (Gen 1-2). The Holy Spirit empowers Jesus, and he proclaims repentance and the kingdom's coming, does good, and heals all those oppressed of the devil (Acts 10:34-38).

We have stated that the gospel is centered in the proclamation of what God has already done in the life, death and resurrection of the Cosmic Crucified. This message is borne and preached by those conformed to the messianic mission of Jesus Christ and rooted in the reality of God, who is creator of heaven and earth. Therefore, the mission of the body of Christ has always been and will always be a mission of word and deed that is passionately concerned about the whole person, the whole community, the restoration of the whole creation.

It is within this context that the church as body of Jesus Christ becomes deeply involved in the totality of human brokenness. The hungry are to be fed, and food is shipped to Ethiopia, southern Sudan, Somalia and Niger where millions of lives are at the edge of starvation. Furthermore, the poor are enabled to develop their own resources so that they may feed themselves, their own families and communities. The oppressed are supported in order that the chains of racism may be broken and all humanity may be free. With and within it all, the gospel of the Cosmic Crucified is always preached in order that all, even the dying and destitute, may live within the incredible costly love and promised victory of God.

It is this struggle to restore the whole of creation that still often leads to contemporary clashes between the kingdom of God and the powers of darkness. Servants are not above their masters. The disciples of Jesus will also meet demonic opposition and be set on trial before priests and kings (Mk 13:9-13).

Churches of the twentieth and 21st centuries clearly have borne the marks of the crucified Jesus. To be baptized or to baptize has meant imprisonment in Nepal. In Sudan Christian villages have been destroyed. Churches speaking for human rights in Central and South America paid an incredible bloody price for their faithful prophetic ministry. Christians who witnessed to the gospel in Eastern Europe before the fall of the Soviet Union forfeited their educational and vocational future. For centuries the Coptic Church of Egypt has lived under Islamic law and rule, which has often discriminated against the minority Christian presence and at times has actually persecuted the Christian community. The Coptic Church understands itself as a martyr church. Prophetic voices like Martin Luther King, Jr., within our own land and our own churches have been ignored, attacked, or socially silenced. The mark of Jesus' cross placed upon the Christian community indicates the costly struggle between the kingdom of God and the realm of darkness. It indicates the Christian community's ongoing participation in this cosmic conflict.

Carl Braaten in *The Apostolic Imperative* writes:

The cross has all too often been cloistered within the Sunday piety of the church, rather than being the dynamic of the everyday soldiers of the cross fighting for justice within the economic, social, and political situations of life.

Although there are other humanitarian groups at work to alleviate suffering and degradation, poverty and hunger, the church will want to be second to none in doing everything within its power to lift the burdens of the million who starve, the races that are humiliated the nations that are held captive, [and] the classes that are deprived of full equality, etc.[106]

Braaten goes on to say that the unique aspect of the church's mission is evangelism, and because no one else will do that, the church must make certain that it does.

It is the messianic restoration of the totality of creation which is the heart of the mission of God.

Costly Discipleship and God's Call to Vulnerability in Mission

God in Christ crucified limits God's messianic, transforming power within history to the power of love which draws and persuades. This assertion is rooted in what God has revealed in the messianic-kingdom mission of the crucified and risen Jesus. Participation in the mission of God's kingdom is participation in God's promised future, which is already present in Jesus Christ.[107] That future of God present in the Cosmic Crucified appears as vulnerable within history. This means that God has not and will not call forth any authoritarian force to protect or enforce God's ultimate messianic mission within history.

[My servant] will not cry or lift up his voice, or make it heard in the street; a bruised reed he will not break, and a dimly burning wick he will not quench; he will faithfully bring forth justice (Is 42:2-3).

This is precisely how the New Testament portrays the mission of the crucified Jesus: prophetic words of grace, challenge and repentance; acts of healing of the sick and exorcism for the captives; banquets with the stigmatized and ostracized; and advocacy for the poor and marginalized. Divine, costly and vulnerable love is present like leaven in a loaf, seeds planted in the ground. The kingdom of God is present but not recognizable unless one has eyes to see and ears to hear.

Participation in the messianic mission of God that actualizes God's future must be conformed to this cruciform, vulnerable, self-giving love manifest in Jesus the Cosmic Crucified. "As the Father has sent me, so I send you" (John 20:19-23). Wesley Ariarajah stated that religious pluralism demands that Christian witness be given in the spirit of one who has truly experienced the humility, the vulnerability and the self-giving that are at the center of Christ's own witness.[108] This study of the biblical faith affirms that the Cosmic Crucified mandates that there is no other way in which any witness to God revealed in the Cosmic Crucified might authentically be given.

This assertion is rooted in the conviction of Jesus Christ's finality and the normativeness of God's incarnation in the Cosmic Crucified for Christian faith and discipleship. As persons grasped by the finality of Jesus Christ, we are told that there is no other way. "If any want to become my followers, let them deny themselves and take up their cross and follow me" (Mk 8:34).

However, in listening to Jesus we are immediately confronted by the absurdity and inadequacy of the church's participation in the cruciform mission of God. The history of the Christian church is replete with examples when the Christian community harassed non-Christians or cooperated with military and social-economic forces to crush the so-called pagan world. From Constantine, who in 312 B.C. placed the sign of the crucified on battle banners; to the Christian Crusades, which fought numerous battles with the Muslim world to retake the "holy city" for Christian worship; to Charlemagne who baptized thousands at the point of the sword; to Ferdinand and Isabella, who threw the Muslim Moors and Jews off the Spanish peninsula; to Columbus and his followers, who on behalf of Europe's leading royal family and the Roman Pope decimated peoples and cultures in the name of the Crucified; to British warships that opened up China's seaports to opium trade and Western missionaries; to twenty-first century America where many Christians find it impossible to witness to Jesus Christ without grafting the Christian message to this nation's concerns about national security and military power — there has existed an overwhelmingly strong element within the Christian community that has refused conformity with the Cosmic Crucified. Many Christians have preferred a theology of glory and a love affair with a triumphant Christendom. The Christian fundamentalist and Zionist, Rev. John Hague, founder of CUFI (Christians United for Israel), is one of the most recent examples of this pagan love affair.

In contrast, there has also been within the Christian community a multitude of Christian witnesses whose message and mission has been conformed to the Cosmic Crucified. They have called people to repentance and proclaimed the compassionate suffering of God and the agonizing, saving death of the Cosmic Crucified one. They have, like Jesus, walked humbly among nations, learning and listening to peoples of every clime and culture. They have healed the sick, made the blind to see and enabled the crippled to walk. They have fed the hungry, clothed the naked and visited the imprisoned. They have advocated for the poor and marginalized. They have done all of these motivated and empowered by God's self-giving, vulnerable, costly love, which has captured their lives by the power of the Holy Spirit. They have gone as participants in God's mission into unknown places and times armed only by the power of the Spirit of God, who has chosen to be vulnerable among us. In participating in the vulnerability of that mission, many have sacrificed their lives and in so doing have participated in Christ's vulnerability unto death. Christ's vulnerability as Lord is our vulnerability as the disciples of the Cosmic Crucified.

The biblical call to conformity with the vulnerability of Jesus crucified raises powerful questions concerning Christian participation in the social and political structures of society. This discussion has particular relevance to our conversations with Muslims, who firmly believe that the power of political structures can or should be used to impose God's will upon the life of the state, and with Buddhists, who have a long tradition of pacifism and non-violence.

Costly Discipleship and Participation in the World of Social and Political Structures

Participation in the messianic mission of the kingdom of God calls for conformity with the self-giving vulnerability of the Cosmic Crucified. Any mission witness to Jesus Christ is molded by the suffering servanthood of Jesus. Does this biblical affirmation preclude Christian participation in political power that imposes by force law and order upon a society?

Questions have been raised as to the relationship between this model for mission and the Christian life in society. For example, does this model for mission imply a Christian pacifism for all of life as argued by John Yoder? He concludes his volume, *The Politics of Jesus*, with this statement:

A social style characterized by the creation of a new community and the rejection of violence of any kind is the theme of the New Testament proclamation from beginning to end, from right to left. The cross of Christ is the model of Christian social efficacy, the power of God for those who believe.[109]

John Yoder reflects an ancient Christian tradition of nonviolence rooted in Jesus' own cruciform ministry. George Forell quotes the early Christian theologian Tertullian (d. 220 C.E.) who argued that Christians could not serve in the imperial army.

> In this context Tertullian addresses the question of Christian service in the military. His answer is eloquent and direct: "There is no agreement between the divine and the human sacrament (*sacramentum* was the military oath of allegiance), the standard of Christ and the standard of the devil, the camp of light and the camp of darkness. One soul cannot belong to two lords—God and Caesar." Noting that on the night of his betrayal Jesus admonished Peter not to defend him with a sword, Tertullian concludes, "The Lord... in disarming Peter, unbelted every soldier!"[110]

This pacifist position reemerged during the time of the Reformation in the nonviolent Anabaptist movement of Menno Simons. John Yoder eloquently represents this tradition.

Following the rise of Constantine to imperial power, the Christian community became more and more identified with the Empire. Forell notes Canon II of the Council of Arles (314 C.E.) "that threatens excommunication to a Christian soldier who throws down his weapons even in times of peace."[111] After Constantine, there emerged a political philosophy and practice that often fused and confused the life and work of church and state in what has been designated Christendom.

Martin Luther in seeking reformation for the church struggled to clarify the roles and relationships between church and state within Christendom. He observed the Roman church functioning like a political institution and attempting to play a political and military role within the Empire. He also observed the Holy Roman Empire interfering and attempting to control the life of the church. As Luther worked to clarify the roles of each to understand the Christian's responsibilities in the world, he spoke of God acting in love through two kingdoms or two ways of reigning in the world.

On the one hand there was the kingdom of God's right hand. Through this reign, which is the power of the gospel, God calls to repentance, proclaims the gospel, and brings forth in the Christian community works of compassion for the neighbor. Complementing the kingdom of the right hand is the kingdom of God's left hand, the law. This work of God is necessary because of sin and rebellion in the world, which are destructive of human life and community. Through God's reign of law with the left hand, God in love holds evil in check and works toward justice. In this kingdom of the left hand, God uses the force of social-political structures, in particular, the "power of the sword."

Luther was convinced that if all persons were true Christians, there would be no need for political structures because all people would spontaneously love their neighbor and walk in the will of God (the Ten Commandments). This would create a society that would be directed for the best advantage for the community. However, this is not the case.

Because society is marked by sin, evil, and forces destructive of life, political structures using force are needed "to preserve peace, punish sin, and restrain the wicked."[112] The Christian "submits most willingly to the rule of the sword, pays his taxes, honors those in authority, serves, helps and does all he can to assist the governing authority that it may continue to function and be held in honor and fear."[113] Furthermore, the Christian should participate in government in order "that the essential governmental authority may not be despised and become enfeebled or perish. For the world cannot and dare not dispense with it".[114] The Christian does this out of love for the sake of the neighbor and others.

Luther recognized that life was incredibly complex. Jesus had said, love your enemies, turn the other cheek, give away your coat, be willing to suffer personal injustice; and Luther believed Christians were called to do this in personal life. However, the Christian, according to love, should not accept injustice for the neighbor. Love may demand justice for the neighbor's sake.

This illustrates one aspect of Luther's two kingdom thought. God in love rules through the gospel in the hearts of people. The same God in love rules the human community through social and political structures for the well-being of the community. Christians participate in both of these activities of God. The two must always be seen in relationship and interacting.[115] In other words, Luther believed God to be extremely well coordinated and ambidextrous.

This Lutheran perspective has been severely criticized because there has been a tendency for Lutherans to say that the church takes responsibility for the gospel and the state takes responsibility for law and order. This has often resulted in the church silently acquiescing to political oppression and injustice.

Carl Braaten in *The Flaming Center* writes, "Our belief is that Lutherans must be willing to take the lead in criticizing this doctrine of two kingdoms, perhaps above all others, because the Lutheran record in applying it on the boundary of church and state stinks with the rotting flesh of human beings in jail and concentration camps."[116] Braaten goes on to a more dialectical treatment of this doctrine, saying yes and no to certain of its elements.[117]

Walter Altmann argues that at his best Luther saw the need for the necessary relationship between the two kingdoms. Altmann recognizes that Luther appeared at times to be subservient to the political authorities, especially the German princes who became protectors and benefactors of the Protestant revolt against Rome. However, Altmann asserts that Luther was a harsh social critic of these powers and illustrates this through Luther's interpretation of Psalm 82:2-4. Altmann writes:

> In his introduction Luther shows how the princes, after having been liberated from the pope's tutelage through the Reformation's proclamation of the gospel, now want to be liberated from the gospel itself in order to, in their turn, be the dominators and even put themselves above God. They want to shut the mouths of the preachers who criticize them, accusing the preachers of being "revolutionaries" and "agitators." But the gospel is revolutionary, and it is part of the preacher's task to denounce that which is evil.[118]

Altmann then summarizes Luther's prophetic message to the princes found in Psalm 82. Luther "distinguishes three tasks: first, to guarantee the free preaching of the gospel, precisely critical and prophetical preaching; second, to defend justice and the rights of the weak and abandoned; and finally, to guarantee the order, peace, and protection of the poor."[119]

Luther was a radical in international politics, advocating a German revolt against the powers of Rome and the Emperor. On the other hand, he proved to be a conservative medieval advocate of law and order in local politics, advocating suppression of the revolting peasants by the princes of the land. Luther was particularly perturbed by the fact that the peasant revolt was being carried out in the name Jesus Christ.

Menno Simons and Martin Luther represent two basic approaches to living out the Christian life within society. Menno Simons believed that conformity to the Cosmic Crucified means that the Christian may not participate in violent imposition of law or the will of God upon people and nations. Christ always calls Christians to transcend violence in their prophetic words and actions intended to establish and preserve justice and peace within the community.

Luther, on the other hand, believed that God and the world of sin and evil required that God work through both gospel and law. God calls Christians to participate in a variety of ways in God's work in the world: preaching of the gospel, works of charity or compassion and non-violent struggles for justice. The work of God's right hand is always carried out within the context of the vulnerability of love. However, for Luther the preservation of justice for others and peace for the nation often require that love sacrifice vulnerability in order to be effective in preserving life within a suffering, broken world.

There is never a question as to how Jesus Christ is to be presented in a world that does not know Christ. There is no question as to how those who preach the Cosmic Crucified are to bear that message into a world of religious pluralism. The message is to be molded by the cross. The message is Jesus crucified, which message is to be carried by Christian witnesses who are willing to be vulnerable until death. The message is to be in words and actions that proclaim and manifest the gracious unconditional love of God. The gospel will be preached, the hungry will be fed, the sick healed and justice advocated in Jesus name.

However, when the new Christian community emerges, the question is raised, "What is their responsibility within their own world?" Will their lives always be molded by love vulnerable to death, or does God call the Christian community to full participation in political structures that could not survive unless the invulnerability of force is applied? There have always been Christians who have insisted that those called by Christ are called to live in Christ's new future messianic age, which in Christ is already present within the old age dominated by conflict, rebellion and hate. They believe that Christians are called to live with and in Christ in vulnerability to death as signs and promises of God's promised future.

Other Christians have argued that as we live between the times, we are in Christ called to participate in the future through gospel-life; however, the powers of the old and present age that threaten human existence must be limited and controlled in order to sustain human community. Christians therefore are paradoxically called to be signs of God's gospel promise and also participants in God's work of the law, preserving life in the present age threatened by the evil of social chaos.[120]

There are other approaches to Christian responsibility in the world. Many Christians have been willing to simply use the power of the state or the militant power of social revolutionary groups to attempt to impose the kingdom of Christ on society. One thinks of the monarchs Constantine and Charlemagne as well as Müntzer, militant Christian Marxist revolutionaries and 21st century U.S. Fundamentalists who pray for an American Christian Theocracy. Questions of religion and state continue to be a major discussion within the Christian community, and it is also a major discussion in the dialogue between major religious traditions. Islam is very straightforward in insisting that Allah wills that the Muslim community actively work to impose the law of Allah (*Sharia*) upon society.

I once spoke to a group of seminary students about Christian witness within the Muslim world. I had focused on the necessity of a ministry carried out in conformity to the Cosmic Crucified. During the discussion period a Nigerian professor asked how I thought the Christian community in Nigeria should respond in the midst of tension and clashes between Muslims and Christians in northern Nigeria. He said our people are tired of being told "to turn the other cheek, because we have already done that more than once." He raises a crucial question about Christian responsibility in a nation which is approximately evenly divided between the two faiths and also constitutionally mandated to preserve religious plurality. Do Christians rally their military and political forces and launch a defense against Muslim militants? Do Christians molded by the Cosmic Crucified continue to witness in a love that is vulnerable to death? Do Christians call upon all responsible citizens to uphold the constitutional guarantees of religious freedom and actively participate in the military and police power that may or may not preserve those constitutional rights?

For the Nigerian Christian churches it is a crucial debate; and unless Nigeria is an exception to Christian history, Christians will come to a variety of conclusions. Some will advocate that disciples of the Cosmic Crucified should live out Christ-like nonviolence and as such be signs of the future. They may struggle for human rights, but they will be militant pacifists. Others will call for Christian responsibility under constitutional law. That may mean active participation in politics, the police and the military. There will also be others who in the name of the crucified one will exploit the frustration and traditional ethnic rivalries present in Nigeria, harnessing the prejudice and hatred of centuries, in order to fight a war of vengeance for the sake of a future Christian majority state. I believe that one can think with "the mind of Christ" about the first two alternatives. The third is clearly a denial of the lordship of the Cosmic Crucified.

I am increasingly convinced that Jesus' call to non-violence and to an allegiance that transcends our national identity must mold our lives. We must be advocates of a militant pacifism which struggles for righteousness and justice with swords that have already been transformed into plowshares. If we at times are convinced in "supreme emergencies" that we are compelled to do otherwise, we cannot claim to resort to military weaponry in the name of Jesus or what Jesus proclaimed as the coming Kingdom of God.[121]

Excursus

It is essential that this reflection on discipleship be read in the context of the previous discussion which affirmed the normative nature of God's revelation in Jesus Christ. Our presentation has affirmed that the essence of God's love will never be other than God's love concretized in Jesus. One can and does trust that the whole of life and the universe are immersed in that love and may be "hoped in" even when galaxies flame out or disappear in black holes of galatic mystery. However, it is even more important in our contemporary context, where much of Christianity in our society perverts the Good News, to affirm the normativeness of Jesus for our discipleship. The primacy of God and the whole human race are central to the mission and message of Jesus. This affirmation of faith is often replaced by the primacy of the nation, national security, the U.S. flag and patriotism. The Pledge of Allegiance makes a greater claim on much of the church than does our Christian identity proclaimed in our baptism. Furthermore, the call of Jesus to participate in the Kingdom of God concretized in Jesus is violated by preachers promising that God is committed to blessing Christians with success, wealth and power. In a pagan "Christian" society where preachers call for violent military attacks on the enemy or make millions of dollars by promising millions of blessings, our call as disciples is to be conformed to Jesus crucified as the absolute norm for our life with God.

It is significant that in the pluralism debate Paul Knitter found it necessary to reject his non-normative Christology position for a number of reasons. The most important was that a relativistic theology left the faith community in a moral wasteland where no criteria for truth and right were present. For Knitter's journey see Appendix II, 229 ff. Knitter concludes with a multi-normed religious world where divine revelation will not contradict itself. For my description and analysis see Appendix II.

Chapter 5

Dialogue and Witness Among Buddhists and Muslims

The discussion of dialogue and witness must be understood within the previous discussion concerning the Jesus crucified and the mission of the church. Earlier in this discussion we noted Wesley Ariarajah's critique of past Christian attempts at dialogue and witness. Ariarajah asserted that these initiatives began with the Christian community making exclusive claims for Jesus Christ and (contrary to Jesus' own ministry of self-giving, unconditional, vulnerable love) resulted in Christian arrogance and intolerance.

The thesis of this book is that the Christian community does make normative affirmations concerning Jesus as the Christ. These affirmations center in the fact that it is the self-giving, unconditionally loving, vulnerable crucified Jesus who concretizes the Kingdom of God. The Christian community affirms that it is precisely the crucified servant of God and Prince of Peace who transcends cultural and historical relativity. We then have explored some of the implications of the Cosmic Crucified for the mission of the church—that is, what does it mean to follow the crucified Jesus who from God's right hand says, "But you will receive power when the Holy Spirit has come upon you; and you will be my witnesses in Jerusalem, in all Judea and Samaria, and to the ends of the earth" (Acts 1:8)? It is now necessary to look for the specific implications of this missiology of the cross for our mission of dialogue and witness.

Sharing the "Good News" (Gospel)

First, the dialogue and witness of the body of Christ will include an awe-filled account of God's incredibly costly and pain-filled entry into human life "in order that all might be saved and come to the knowledge of the truth (1 Tm 2:4)." In joy-filled wonder, the disciples of Jesus Christ will search the languages and cultures of the cosmos in order to witness faithfully to the awesome wonder that in Jesus, God was with us and in Jesus God was concretized as revealer of transforming truth.

Christian participation in dialogue and witness begins within the context of this faith. One of the primary implications of this vision is that every person, whether Christian, Muslim or Buddhist, is unconditionally and passionately loved by that Ultimate Reality at the heart of the universe. Every person met within every engagement of dialogue and witness has cosmic value and infinite worth. One is called to value those of such worth by listening to them and caring about them.

Crucified Minds

Second, the dialogue and witness of the body of Christ will be conformed to the Cosmic Crucified. "Let the same mind be in you that was in Christ Jesus, who, though he was in the form of God, did not regard equality with God as something to be exploited, but emptied himself, taking the form of a slave..." (Phil 2:5ff). In the words of Kosuke Koyama, the Christian witness moves into the world with crucified minds. Authentic witness to Jesus Christ is borne by joy-filled witnesses humbled by God's incredible and unconditional grace. These disciples are called by the crucified and empowered by the Spirit to be conformed to the self-giving, vulnerable love of God in their witness.

They will walk in the baptismal promise of grace through which God in Christ daily cleanses of all sin. Daily they will hear Jesus say, Die to that which does not conform to me and rise to the cruciform mission of the Cosmic Crucified. "Take up your cross and follow me" (Mk 8:34).

Ariarajah is no doubt correct when he notes that the Christian witness has often been arrogant, intolerant and even worse. However, if nothing else, it is hoped that this study has shown that the true recognition of the lordship of Jesus crucified will lead to humble, self-giving, vulnerable servanthood rather than to the opposite. Most of us will recognize that the Christian community is the first to be called to repentance and renewal in the presence of the Cosmic Crucified. If our message and mission are not conformed to Jesus as Christ, then we are in danger of replicating the mission of some of Jesus' contemporaries who, Jesus claimed, crossed sea and land to make a single convert only to make them children of hell like themselves (Mt 23:15).

Participants in Divine Compassion

Third, the dialogue and witness of the body of Christ is rooted in God's suffering-with-us love that is divine compassion. Dialogue and witness begin with the assumption that God is already present and in solidarity with Buddhists and Muslims and has already seen their affliction, heard their cries and knows their suffering. Dialogue and witness conformed to Jesus crucified is compelled to be a suffering-with-us dialogue and witness—a presence of solidarity with people, with their joys and sorrows, hopes and crushed dreams.

On January 19, 1992, Dr. Albert Glock, an ELCA missionary, was murdered near Birzeit University on the West Bank. Glock was a professor of archeology at Birzeit University. He had begun his career like most Western biblical archaeologists, exploring the ancient civilizations of the Middle East. However, he became aware of the fact that there was little concern for the last 500 years or 1,000 years when the land was inhabited by the Palestinian Arab peoples. He saw this history ignored as recent history was scraped away to plumb the culture of the times of Abraham, David, Jeremiah, or the Maccabees. In that process, he saw one more attempt to deny a Palestinian people their own history and tradition. With that concern primary in his mind, he gave his life to enabling Palestinian people to discover through archeology their own place within the history of the nations. Glock and his wife Lois literally chose to be in solidarity with a suffering and exploited people, both Muslim and Christian. The suffering-with-us God had called Al and Lois to be participants in the suffering-with-us body of Christ. "If one member suffers, all suffer together with it" (1 Cor 12:26). All authentic dialogue and witness begins in solidarity with people in their joys and in their pain.

Participants in the Messianic Struggle

Fourth, dialogue and witness is rooted in God's messianic struggle with the powers of darkness that distort and destroy God's creation and God's creative intentions for life filled with compassion, justice and peace. When faithful to their call the Jesus people have been advocates of the abolition of slavery; they have struggled for the liberation of women from cultural and societal prisons; they have worked for the elimination of poverty; they have lived and preached forgiveness for "the damned"; they have placed center-stage the marginalized whether slave or gay; and they have empowered and transformed the "nobodies" of the world. They have renounced and denounced violence, greed, oppression and hypocrisy: in doing so they have been despised and rejected by their contemporaries in societies. Persons cruciformed by the Cosmic Crucified will be participants in this divine struggle for compassion, justice and peace.

Christians engaged with Muslim and Buddhist communities will encounter people who also struggle for compassion, justice and peace. Muslims believe that Allah wills that all creation surrender to the will of Allah and therein find justice and peace. Buddhists understand their eight-fold path to *nirvana* as including a walk of compassion, justice and peace. In spite of these differing perspectives, Christians, Muslims and Buddhists have shared problems, struggles and dreams that necessitate shared strategies on behalf of life.

Conversations in Behalf of a Common Life

Fifth, authentic interfaith dialogue or conversations must begin with mutual conversations between Christian and Buddhists or Christian and Muslims concerning the value and meaning of life; the brokenness and suffering as well as the joys of people; the common visions and struggles for compassion, justice and peace. As Christians, we are called to carry on those conversations within the call of the Cosmic Crucified to love and serve unconditionally all people regardless of nationality, race, or religious identity, even if it means someone designated "the enemy."

"You have heard that it was said, 'You shall love your neighbor and hate your enemy.' But I say to you, Love your enemies and pray for those who persecute you, so that you may be children of your Father in heaven; for he makes his sun rise on the evil and on the good, and sends rain on the righteous and on the unrighteous. For if you love those who love you, what reward have you? Do not even the tax collectors do the same? And if you greet only your brothers and sisters, what more are you doing than others? Do not even the Gentiles do the same? Be perfect, therefore, as your heavenly Father is perfect." (Mt 5:43-48)

Significantly, the Qur'an in Surah 5:48 reads:

And to you [O Muhammad!] We have sent down the Book in truth as a confirmer of the Books [i.e., all Revelations] that have come before it and as a protector over them... For each one of you [Jews, Christians, Muslims], We have appointed a path and a way, and if God had so willed, He would have made you but one community but [He has not done so in order] that He try [all of] you in what He has given you; *wherefore compete with one another in good deeds...*[122] (emphasis added).

Theological dialogue or Christian-Muslim conversations should take place within these broader conversations and shared struggles for life. Within this context, the possibility exists for mutual respect and mutual understanding. Only as people live with and for each other can honest conversations take place concerning one another's deepest religious convictions, clarifying how each of us understands life and faith similarly and/or differently.

The Necessity of Witness and Dialogue for Muslims, Buddhists and Christians

Within this context one can begin to discuss one of the more controversial questions concerning the purpose of Christian mission among Buddhists and Muslims. Is the purpose of Christian mission among Buddhists and Muslims a dialogue through which clarity and mutual enrichment can take place? Or is the purpose of mission also grounded in the hope that Buddhists and Muslims eventually might be touched by God's grace spoken and embodied in Jesus? This presentation argues that it will be both.

Necessary Witness

Christianity, Islam and Buddhism have been missionary in nature. Although there are exceptions, members of these religious communities have believed that they are called to give witness to the form of faith that has grasped them. By their very nature these communities desire to share what they believe to be the word of truth to humanity. Gautama Buddha chose to share the truth of liberation with his disciples, and *bodhisattvas*, particularly within Mahayana Buddhism, renounce their crossing to *nirvana* in order to share the truth of their journey with suffering humanity. Muslims from the time of Muhammed have understood themselves to be vice-regents of God who are called to bring Allah's will into every dimension of life. Jesus knew himself as sent from God to preach repentance and incorporation into the new life of the kingdom of God. In turn, the Christ sends his disciples into the world: "As the Father has sent me, even so I send you" (John 20:21). When Buddhists, Muslims and Christians meet, our traditions call all of us to witness. If any of us denies this, we deny our existence as a people who believe that we are captured by authentic truth to be shared with suffering people.

Dialogue for Listening — Affirmation, Understanding and Enrichment

Dialogue is first participation in God's self-giving and vulnerable love for people. Divine love always includes concern for the value and well-being of the one loved and necessarily affirms the other. Love affirms people, creating "somebodies" out of "nobodies."

One of the most powerful ways that love affirms people is by listening to them. Listening to a person values and respects the inner life and being of the other. Vulnerable love goes further and through listening is willing to receive and value the inner life of the other, even though it may sound strange and dissident. Dialogue in participation with the Cosmic Crucified necessitates listening love as affirmation and respect of someone created in the image of God and someone for whom God in Christ suffered and is suffering.

The possibility of witnessing, which all three traditions call for and desire, can take place only if Buddhists, Muslims and Christians actually understand each other. Authentic Christian witness among Buddhists depends on Buddhists actually hearing the biblical witness to Jesus. Authentic Muslim witness among Christians depends on Christians actually hearing the message of Muhammad. In order to understand another person's faith and effectively witness to Jesus crucified, it is essential to attempt to understand the faith of Muslims and Buddhists as they believe it should be understood.

There are innumerable barriers to this sharing of faith through witness. The centuries of separation and alienation demand that the Christian community take absolutely seriously the cruciform mission of the church within the Muslim and Buddhist world. Furthermore, the centuries of religious and theological misunderstanding demand that patient in-depth dialogue always be the context for witness to the faith.

Since persons of faith and rich religious traditions are found within Christian, Muslim and Buddhist communities, sincere and honest dialogue cannot be anything other than enriching. John B. Cobb, Jr. in his book *Beyond Dialogue* states that dialogue between

Buddhists and Christians has possibilities for mutual enrichment and what he calls mutual transformation as dialogue enables all participants to see their own vision from new and valuable perspectives.[123]

Implications of the Biblical Inclusive Theme for Dialogue and Witness

Contemporary theology as articulated by Hick, Ariarajah and Knitter is marked by a universalism that challenges the nature of Christian witness among peoples of other faiths. As noted earlier, religious pluralism often assumes that God is universally present and God's revelation and/or saving power are universally present to the whole human community. Religious pluralism also assumes that there are numerous revelations of God that reveal who God is and what God thinks and does. A third presupposition of religious pluralism claims that all of these revelations are in some sense authentic, and none of them is the normative revelation by which all other revelatory claims are to be critiqued. The bottom line for this position is that Jesus is one among many revelatory events. The human challenge is to seek through Jesus and all these revelatory events for an understanding of the ultimate mystery within the universe. In Hindu terms, we are all on paths toward God's truth, and meaningful conversations will facilitate our common human journey.

We have not followed that path; however, we have noted the importance of God's presence and revelation within every people and their culture. God is universally present to the whole of creation and to the whole human family. That is clearly a major biblical theme, manifest in God's creation and care of the whole universe (Gen 1); God's universally present wisdom, which works within human personalities and structures (Prb 8; Rom 2); God's covenant through Noah with the entire human family (Gen 9); God's call of Abraham and Israel for the blessing of all the nations of the earth (Gen 12, Isaiah 42 and 49); God's planting of the human search for God within all people (Acts 17); and God's plan to recreate and restore all of creation (1 Cor 15:20-28; Eph 1:9-10; Phil 2:9-11). Within the biblical accounts this universal presence and wisdom of God is seen in concrete people outside the household of the biblical faith such as Melchizedek (Gen 14), Jethro (Ex 18), Ruth, Job, the Roman centurion (Mt 8:5-13), the Syrophoenician woman (Mk 7:24-30). Jesus pointed to the same universal reality in his parable of the Good Samaritan (Lk 10:25-37) and in his announcement that, "Many will come from east and west and sit at table with Abraham, Isaac, and Jacob in the kingdom of heaven, while the sons of the kingdom will be thrown into the outer darkness" (Mt 8:11-12).

This biblical theme is supported by the universal Christian experience that continually encounters persons of integrity and authentic openness to God's will and truth outside our own religious tradition. At times one finds persons who have understood the mission and message of Jesus with far greater depth than most Christians. M. K. Gandhi, the Hindu Indian advocate of nonviolence, is certainly one of those persons. Gandhi writes of Jesus:

> What then does Jesus mean to me? To me he was one of the greatest teachers humanity has ever had. To his believers, he was God's only begotten Son. Could the fact that I do or do not accept this belief make Jesus any more or less an influence in my life? Is all the grandeur of his teaching and doctrine to be forbidden to me? I cannot believe so. To me it implies a spiritual birth. My interpretation, in other words, is that in Jesus' own life is the key to the nearness of God: that he expressed as no other could the spirit and will of God. It is in this sense that I see him and recognize him as the Son of God.[124]

As Christians, we are called in our dialogue and witness to take this biblical affirmation of God's universal, cosmic presence and revelation seriously. We will always be looking for the footprints of God in people's lives. As we listen to people who are created in the image of God (Gen 1:26) and who are bought with the price of the pain of God incarnate in the Cosmic Crucified, we will listen for insights into that which is good, beautiful and true—the will of God.

Recognition of sin as human brokenness and rebellion will prevent us from idealistic naiveté that glosses over what is distorted in human lives, cultures and religions. However, in dialogue and witness, one is called to look for the best in other people's lives and faiths. One who believes that God's final truth is concretized in the Jesus crucified will not find it necessary to berate another person's faith in order to make Jesus Christ "look good."

The Christian rests in the trust that there is no past or future revelation of God that will negate the hope in the Cosmic Crucified; namely, that at the heart of the universe is the God willing to share human existence, solidarity with pain and brokenness, and in concretized form as Jesus go through struggling, suffering, and death for humanity's sake. This will always be the heart of our Christian witness.

Chapter 6

The Unique Theological Task in Engaging with Muslim Peoples

In 1960 Daud Rahbar, a Muslim scholar, published a book entitled *God of Justice*.[125] In it, he argued that Allah as revealed in the Qur'an was not a *"capricious tyrant"* as some non-Muslims charged, but rather was the God of justice.[126] The book reflects a careful study of the Qur'an supporting this thesis. Fazlur Rahman makes a similar statement in his well-known book, *Major Themes of the Qur'an*, where he states "the ultimate reality... is conceived in Islam as *merciful justice* rather than fatherhood" (emphasis added) as in Christianity.[127] Christians need to note that it is indeed *merciful* justice emphasized by Muslims like Rahman.

Later in his life Daud Rahbar became attracted to Jesus. He was asked what had drawn him to Jesus? In his autobiography he replies to this question. In a short statement recounting why he found Jesus significant, he comments that humanity searches for the "worshipable," and his autobiographical sketch portrays a Muslim in search of that which is worthy of worship and adoration.[128] As a Muslim, he had meditated upon the ultimate mystery and nature of Allah who was Allah *akbar*, that is, "God is greater," greater than any human conception. No predicate is adequate to describe the ultimate wonder of God. One thinks of Anselm's definition of God as that "than which nothing greater can be conceived." Like every Muslim, Daud Rahbar had daily prayed with his forehead on the ground, surrendering himself to Allah (*Islam* literally meaning "to surrender") and in that surrender had sought significance and peace for life.

Rahbar then relates that in talking with Christian friends and reading the New Testament he was struck by the account of Jesus' self-giving love and his sacrificial death (most Muslims do not ac-

Engaging with Muslim Peoples • **99**

cept the reality of Jesus' death). In this self-giving, suffering love, Rahbar says he encountered a most excellent love, "a love worthy of the eternal God." He was grasped by that love and concluded that this most excellent love must be of God.

Fazlur Rahman, the outstanding Muslim scholar, however, sees Christianity's focus upon sacrificial love as a major weakness within the Christian faith. In contrast to Rahbar, he writes, "But such religious ideologies as have put their whole emphasis upon God's love and self-sacrifice for the sake of His children have done little service to the moral maturity of man."[129] Rahman asks when is man to become responsible for his own life, when is he to come of age?[130]

Costly Grace and Merciful Justice

After a talk in which I had told the story of Daud Rahbar, a Muslim, Amin, came up to me and said, "I don't think you interpreted Islam correctly because you did not explain that Muslims also believe in a merciful, forgiving God as well as a God of justice." I apologized to him and said that I would like to talk with him about his understanding of justice and mercy. After a lengthy discussion, we agreed that Muslims look at mercy through the lens of justice, while Christians look at justice through the lens of mercy as costly grace. During a later session, Amin was asked to give his interpretation of Islam to the group.

After his presentation, he was asked whether Muslims believed that God would always forgive. He replied that he did not think that forgiveness in every case would be possible because justice might be violated. He thought that from the perspective of Islam, Allah would take into account every person's total life. Allah would certainly be mercifully forgiving; however, that forgiveness could not be unconditional. Forgiveness and mercy would be limited by God's concern for justice.

Fazlur Rahman, recognized as one of the most distinguished interpreters of Islam, speaks in similar terms. Interpreting the Qur'an, Rahman writes: "Several other verses also indicate that God will pardon or overlook men's lapses, provided the overall performance is good and beneficial."[131] Surah 4:31 reads: "If you avoid the major evils that have been prohibited you, we shall obliterate occasional and smaller lapses."[132] Rahman's perspective views merciful justice at the heart of Islam and is seen as the impetus for humanity's moral growth and maturity.[133]

Dr. G. H. Aasi, Professor of Islamic Studies at the American Islamic College in Chicago and a teaching colleague at the Lutheran School of Theology at Chicago, believes that Rahman represents a school of thought which has an emphasis on justice. Dr. Aasi argues that limiting God's mercy is clearly against the Quranic message. He points to Surah 7.156 where the Quran reads, "But my mercy extendeth (overspreads) to all things" and Surah 6.12 and 54: "Allah has inscribed for Himself (binds Himself) to mercy." Mercy rather than justice has the priority.

In contrast to Islam's merciful justice as presented by Fazlur Rahman, the Christian message centers in the costly unconditional love of God. When reflecting upon life, Daud Rahbar stated that "the paradox of God's mercy and justice troubled me and that I wanted to relate to God on terms of His unconditional mercy."[134] As Christians engage with persons of other faiths, they will find that the gospel is unique in proclaiming the costly suffering grace—vulnerability unto death—present in the Jesus crucified.

The outstanding Christian interpreter of Islam, Kenneth Cragg writes, "At the heart of 'the gospel of the blessed God' is a proven divine capacity to love and the cross is where we can know it so. There too is a bearing of evil which is a bearing away of it.... It is an acknowledgment which Christian thought and experience find the more authentic as *awareness of other faiths makes its distinctiveness the more compelling*" [135] (emphasis added).

While teaching in Nigeria in the 1960s, I met a Pakistani Muslim, Azmi, who became a good friend. He was a man of deep devotion, literally surrendering every detail of his life to the will of God. From his five daily prayers commanded by the Qur'an to the shape of his beard, which he found in the *hadith*, or the traditions concerning Muhammad, Azmi lived in conformity to the will of Allah. He was also a zealous witness to his faith, continually talking to his students and friends about the richness of the Islamic tradition.

One day as we shared dinner, he said, "You know I have a recurring dream. I am standing at the edge of an abyss. Allah awaits on the other side as my judge. The only way that I may cross is to walk on a narrow rope, and I am falling off." Does Allah wait in merciful justice energizing our moral responsibility in preparation for Allah's final judgment, as believed by Fazlur Rahman and my friend Azmi? Or does God in suffering, self-giving love cross the abyss to us, bearing responsibility for our relationship with God and promising that our sin and failures can never separate us from the love of God in Christ Jesus?

Fazlur Rahman argues that the Christian focus upon costly grace leads to human irresponsibility. Christians will have to agree that this has often been the case since the times of the Apostle Paul, who wrote: "Should we continue in sin in order that grace may abound?" "By no means!" replies Paul, because the disciples of the Cosmic Crucified are persons conformed to Christ—they are a cruciform people (Rom 6.1-4)!

Christians engaged with Muslims will repeatedly discuss this message of merciful justice and costly grace. They represent different emphases in our traditions. We will also become aware of different perspectives within the Muslim tradition. Dr. Aasi from the American Islamic College is not an isolated voice speaking of the priority of divine mercy but represents an emphasis found in the Islamic spiritual and mystical tradition called Sufism. Our conversations will be the occasion for seeing different perspectives and for mutual enrichment. They may lead us back to Romans 6 and they may draw many of us to a deeper understanding of what it means to be persons drawn to the foot of the cross.

Incarnation and *Shirk*

The Qur'an's basic critique of Christianity is that it has elevated that which is human, Jesus, and has identified Jesus with God.

> O People of the Book!
> Commit no excesses
> In your religion: nor say
> Of Allah aught but the truth.
> Christ Jesus the son of Mary
> Was (no more than)
> A Messenger of Allah.
> And His Word,
> Which He bestowed on Mary,
> And a Spirit proceeding
> From Him: so believe
> In Allah and His Messengers.
> Say not "Trinity:" desist:
> It will be better for you:
> For Allah is one God:
> Glory be to Him:

(Far Exalted is He) above
Having a son. To Him
Belong all things in the heavens
And on the earth. And enough
Is Allah as a Disposer of affairs.[136]

Fazlur Rahman writes: "You may not point to any human being, with delimitations and a date of birth, and say simply, 'that person is God.' To the Qur'an, this is neither possible, nor intelligible, nor pardonable."[137] Rahman also states: "In any case, the unacceptability of Jesus' divinity and the Trinity to the Qur'an is incontrovertible."[138] For Islam there is an infinitude about the reality of God that no element of creation shares. "It is precisely this belief in such sharing [creaturehood participating in Godhood] that is categorically denied by the Qur'anic doctrine of *shirk* or 'participation in Godhead.'"[139]

It has often been noted that Muhammad probably encountered a form of Christianity that associated Jesus and Mary with God in a manner not acceptable to orthodox Christian teaching and that similar non-orthodox views continue within the Christian community today. No matter where that discussion leads, Islam does raise the question as to whether the Christian faith affirms, as it desires, monotheism. Is Christian conversation concerning the Trinity a unique manner of affirming the unity of God, or is it a deterioration of monotheism into tritheism? Christians would affirm the former; Muslims are convinced of the latter. This will necessarily be a major discussion whenever Muslims and Christians dialogue.

From the Christian perspective, three basic principles have led the Christian community to speak of the incarnation and Trinity, and all three arise out of Christian convictions concerning God's revelation. First is the resurrection of Jesus from the dead. This event is God's declaration that God's will has been spoken and lived in the life of Jesus of Nazareth. In the words of Robert Jenson, quoted earlier, "Only the resurrection of the dead will verify Yahweh's self-introduction as God."[140]

There is a second principle that lies behind the Christian affirmation of the incarnation. The principle is the affirmation that God moves into history and human lives to reveal and speak God's word. The form of biblical revelation is strikingly different from the form of Qur'anic revelation. From a Muslim perspective, the Qur'an is Allah's Arabic verbal message given to Muhammad to be recited for

God's people. Allah speaks; Muhammad recites. Some biblical prophetic passages are understood in this way. For example, "The word that came to Jeremiah from the Lord: Stand in the gate of the Lord's house, and proclaim there this word, and say, Hear the word of the Lord" (Jer 7:1-2).

The biblical message, however, takes many other forms, such as prayers and hymns from people's hearts, documented history, biographical accounts of prophets lives, letters and Gospels. Here God speaks within and through human lives and experiences. As God's word is communicated through the lives and history of a people, God is the suffering-with-us God, the God who, for example, is intimately wrapped up in the marriage of Hosea the prophet (Hosea 1-3) or the return from exile by the people of Judah (Isaiah 40ff). God speaks in Hosea's painful experience of an unfaithful wife and in the life of his suffering servant people and prophet. God's activity and speech are so intimately involved in the life of God's prophets and people that God's Word passes into the very being of the prophet. Terence Fretheim writes, "In some sense God takes up 'residence' in the very life of the prophet. The prophet becomes a vehicle of divine immanence."[141]

Fretheim concludes his essay: "Finally, we should note that the prophet's life as embodied word of God is partial and broken. The [Old Testament] does not finally come to the conclusion that God was incarnate in a human life in complete unbrokenness or in its entirety. The word of God enfleshed in an unbroken way in the totality of a human life must await a new day. Yet, in the prophet we see decisive continuities with what occurs in the Christ-event. God's act in Jesus Christ is the culmination of a long-standing relationship of God with the world that is more widespread in the OT than is commonly recognized."[142]

For the Christian community, Jesus the crucified is the incarnation of God, the suffering-with-us God. Here in this personality the Word of God is fully expressed. Kenneth Cragg writes: "Whereas the ultimate speech of God for Islam is prophecy, 'sealed,' as the phrase goes, or accomplished, in Muhammad, the speech of God for the Christian is personality . . . the Person of Jesus Christ in the flesh."[143]

Willem A. Bijlefeld in his essay "Christian Witness in an Islamic Context" observes that in contrast to the Christian perspective outlined by Fretheim, Muslim thinkers have advocated that revelation is not intimately related to history; it is rather a-temporal and a-historical as God's Word from eternity strikes into the temporal. Any other form of revelation from a Muslim perspective compromises the nature of Allah. "The whole issue of 'God and history' would seem to be one of the major points for Christian-Muslim conversations and reflections."[144]

Kenneth Cragg suggests that Christians raise with Muslims the question as to whether one limits the sovereignty of God by prescribing what is possible for the reality of God:

> Must God not be left to determine the steps of the divine purpose and shall we say no? If so, then we can never say that the Incarnation could not be. If it cannot be denied as a possibility, then any claims of occurrence cannot be ruled out in advance. They must be investigated as a matter of historical evidence. Such investigation brings us back to Christ in human history.[145]

Third, the impelling principle that has driven the Christian community to speak of Christ as the incarnation of God is a response to the question as to whether God in revelation may be other than God who is the revealer. This was a question raised within the early church as it moved into the Hellenistic culture of the Roman Empire. Within the early Aramaic-speaking church, it was possible to confess the finality of Jesus the Cosmic Crucified in messianic terms. Jesus as Messiah fulfilled all the promises of God that had been envisioned by the Old Testament prophets. The early church assumed that God, the ultimate reality, was present within Israel and by the power of the Holy Spirit was active for the restoration of all creation. The Spirit had inspired the prophets, created the Messiah in Mary's womb, empowered the messianic mission of Jesus, raised Jesus from the dead, and was poured out upon the early church. There was no question within the early church that when one encounters Jesus crucified one encountered the reality and power of God. There was no question as to whether one met the revealer in the revelation; whether God ultimately might be other than God was in Jesus the crucified, risen and returning Messiah.

Within Hellenistic culture it was otherwise. The world of spiritual being in the Hellenistic world was hierarchical, and at the apex of that world of the divine was the ultimate—the One. This ultimate One was totally transcendent having no possibility of being related to lower realms of spirit, much less to the physical world of body and soul. The early Christian Arians taught that the Word of

God incarnate in Jesus was a reality other than the Ultimate One. The *logos* that became incarnate was a second God created by and different from the Ultimate One.

They had views that Fazlur Rahman states would have been more acceptable to the Qur'an. Rahman writes, "The Qur'an would most probably have no objections to the Logos having become flesh if the Logos were not simply identified with God and the identification were understood less literally."[146]

The Nicene fathers thought that such a theological development engendered by the influence of Greek philosophy threatened the very essence of Christianity because it asserted that the Reality revealed and encountered in Jesus was different from God and therefore not the same as God. One would always question whether one day God might act and be revealed in a totally different manner from what one encountered in Jesus Christ. God might not be the one who willed to be vulnerable even unto death for the sake of humanity. The Nicene confessionalists therefore insisted that Jesus is God, Light of Light, very God of very God. One could trust that God is trustworthy. There is, nor would be, no other God than the Ultimate Reality concretized in Jesus.[147]

When Christian-Muslim discussions focus on the preexistence of the Word which became flesh in Jesus Christ (John 1:1-14) or upon the divine nature of Christ, it may be noted that similar discussions have taken place within the Muslim community concerning the Qur'an. The Mutazilites (ninth century) argued that the Qur'an was created by God. They debated with those who argued that the Qur'an was eternal sharing the perfection of God's speech. The Mutazilites were concerned that a form of Qur'anic incarnationalism would slip into Islam. Eventually the understanding of the Qur'an as eternal was accepted within the Muslim community. Christians may appeal to this tradition as a way of making some analogies concerning the pre-existence and divinity of the Cosmic Crucified.[148]

The Christian community wishes to say that statements concerning the incarnation are statements of the unity of God. There is one God who is Revealer (Father), Revelation (Son incarnate) and Revealedness (the Spirit of Father and Son who enlightens and empowers the body of Christ in God's mission in the world).[149]

This affirmation of the unity of God may not be that which Muslims deny. Some Christians may agree when the Qur'an states that Jesus will be asked on the Day of Judgment whether he had taught trinitarianism to his followers, and he shall reply, "Glory be to Thee! Never could I say what I had no right (to say). Had I said such a thing, Thou wouldst Indeed have known it" (Surah 5:116). A trinitarian affirmation of God's unity is not rooted in Jesus' own words but in the church's convictions concerning the cosmic finality of Jesus Christ, and how that finality needed to be expressed in a Hellenistic culture that questioned the capacity of the "Highest God" to be passionately wrapped up in human existence.

Fazlur Rahman quotes the Qur'anic invitation to community within the unity of God: "O People of the Book! Let us come together upon a formula which is common between us—that we shall not serve anyone but God, that we shall associate none with Him" (Surah 3:64)."[150]

Christians affirm the same unity within the reality of God; however, they see the one God through the window of Jesus the Cosmic Crucified. This is expressed in the early saying of Jesus found in Matthew 11:25-27 and Luke 10:21-24. Through that window faith sees into the heart of the universe, from whence the creator of cosmic unity reintegrates and restores the world through the power of self-giving vulnerability incarnate in the Cosmic Crucified. Christians who acknowledge that ultimate truth will be called by the Triune God into self-giving, vulnerable life conformed to Christ for the sake of God's reconciling mission in the world.

The Vindication of the Prophet

According to most Muslims, the Qur'an states that Jesus did not die on the cross. In Surah 4 a number of charges are brought against the Jewish community, "The people of the Book" who have Moses as prophet (Surah 4:153ff). One of those accusations reads:

> That they said (in boast)
> "We killed Christ Jesus
> The Son of Mary,
> The Messenger of Allah"—
> But they killed him not,
> Nor crucified him,
> But so it was made
> To appear to them, . . .
> For of a surety
> They killed him not—

Nay, Allah raised him up
Unto Himself; and Allah
Is Exalted in Power, Wise-"
(Surah 4:157-158)

Christians must recognize that Muslims deny the crucifixion of Jesus because they recognize Jesus as a messenger of God, and messengers of God are vindicated by God in this life as well as in the Day of Judgment. Dr. Fazlur Rahman writes, "Divine succor and final victory belongs to God's Messengers and those who support them: 'We do, indeed, help our Messengers and the believers in this life as well as on the Day when the Witnesses shall stand up'" (Surah 40:51).[151] Rahman argues that this Qur'anic theme of victory of good over evil leads to the vindication of the Messengers of Allah. Rahman writes:

> It is because of this basic line of thought concerning the final victory of good over evil that the Qur'an refers constantly to the vindication of Noah, who was saved from the flood; of Abraham, who was saved from fire; of Moses, who was saved from Pharaoh and his hordes; and of Jesus, who was saved from execution at the hands of the Jews (hence the rejection by the Qur'an of the crucifixion story). Muhammad must equally be vindicated: he will not only be saved but his Message will be victorious."[152]

From a Muslim perspective, the New Testament account of the crucifixion is corrected to indicate that some unknown person resembling Jesus was put to death in his stead. From a Christian perspective, Kenneth Cragg writes that Islam has robbed Jesus of his own identity as the Christ Crucified. "The Jesus of the Gospels is undiscernible in the shadowy figure who is made to quit the path of his own teaching ['the Son of Man must suffer'] and his own *islam*, or 'surrender,' to the redeeming purpose of God. Truly here at the Muslim Cross we must say, as was said of old: 'They know not what they do.'"[153]

The understanding of the suffering of God and Jesus' crucifixion is the crucial parting of the ways between Christians and Muslims. For Muslims the suffering and death of Allah's Messenger is not appropriate to God's presence and action, God's power and glory. God "cannot be thought not to rescue his servant from the hands of his enemies."[154] From the Muslim perspective, vulnerability unto death is not appropriate for the kingdom/reign of God. The Christian faith asserts precisely the opposite; namely, that God has chosen in the

Cosmic Crucified to be vulnerable even unto death. This divine vulnerability even unto death is the very ground of our salvation.

This discussion clarifies for both Muslims and Christians how we believe in one God differently. "We are left with simple witness and the conviction we cannot enforce but only affirm that 'God was in Christ reconciling the world unto himself.'"[155]

Islam and Social-Political Structures

The origins of Islam, unlike Christianity, are traced to revelation given to a person who was recognized not only as a prophet but also as a community statesman.[156] Muhammad's prophetic ministry began in the city of Mecca; however, due to opposition to his work, Muhammad and his followers moved to Medina (622 C.E.). In Medina, Muhammad became the leader of a social-political community, and the revelatory messages received by Muhammad were filled with divine directives concerning community life.

Fazlur Rahman writes: "There is no doubt that the Qur'an wanted Muslims to establish a political order on earth for the sake of creating an egalitarian and just moral-social order."[157] Muslims inevitably integrate religion and social-political order because the Qur'an, as Allah's revelation, integrates all of life, individual and corporate, under the will of Allah.

Nations as well as individuals are called to submission to the will of God. H. A. R. Gibb writes that this original integration of religion and social-political life in Muhammad's life remained a basic motif within the Muslim community down through its history. "The connection between law and religion thus established by Mohammed and adopted by his followers persisted throughout all later centuries."[158]

Revelation is the grounds for the social-political order. The Qur'anic revelation supplemented by the *Hadith* (the traditions focused upon Muhammad) and later Muslim legal interpretations of the revelatory base are to be the legal basis for Muslim people. This totality is designated *Sharia*, the law. How then does the community as a nation endeavor to live in conformity to the will of Allah and to seek that Allah's will be done on earth? This is essential because the Muslim community is "charged with 'being witnesses upon mankind' and 'calling to goodness and prohibiting evil'" (Surah 2:143; 3:104, 110).[159] Fazlur Rahman answers the previous question with the Islamic concept *jihad*, which "is a total endeavor, an all-out effort—'with your wealth and lives,' as the Qur'an frequently puts it—to 'make God's cause succeed'" (Surah 9:40).[160]

Muslims speak of a greater and lesser *jihad.* The greater struggle is the person's inner struggle to live in submission to the will of Allah; the outer struggle is the effort to make God's cause succeed within the corporate society. Muslim peoples and leaders are called to seek the will of God's law in society. Political leaders are to establish worship and pay the poor their due and enjoin kindness and forbid iniquity (Surah 22:41).

Fazlur Rahman addresses Muslims' critics with these fascinating words:

> But when human religio-social endeavor is envisaged in the terms in which we have understood the Qur'an, *jihad* becomes an absolute necessity. How can such an ideological world-order be brought into existence without such a means? Most unfortunately, Western Christian propaganda has confused the whole issue by popularizing the slogan 'Islam was spread by the sword' or 'Islam is a religion of the sword.' What was spread by the sword was not the religion of Islam, but the *political domain* of Islam, so that Islam could work to produce the order on the earth that the Qur'an seeks. One may concede that *jihad* was often misused by later Muslims whose primary aim was territorial expansion and not the ideology they were asked to establish; one must also admit that the means of *jihad* can vary—in fact, armed *jihad* is only one form. But one can never say that 'Islam was spread by the sword.' There is no single parallel in Islamic history to the forcible conversion to Christianity of the German tribes *en masse* carried out by Charlemagne, with repeated punitive expeditions against apostates—although, of course, locally and occasionally isolated cases of such conversions may well have taken place.[161]

As noted above, Islam works "to produce the order on earth that the Qur'an seeks." This concept raises crucial issues wherever Muslims live with non-Muslim minorities or with non-Muslim majorities. In the southern Sudan, Indonesia and Malaysia, minority Christians feel threatened by the imposition or potential imposition of *Sharia.* In Nigeria almost equally large populations of Muslims and Christians debate the role of *Sharia* within constitutional government, and Christians debate their own role within a constitutional state. In India and the U.S.A., minority Muslim populations seek to adapt to a world in which Muslim law cannot function as a political reality; however, some Muslims will see good constitutional law based upon justice as a manifestation of God's law within society.

Rahman wishes to make a distinction between the Muslim religion and the Muslim political domain. He advocates, as the Qur'an does, religious freedom. The Qur'an states, "There is no compulsion in religion" (Surah 2:256). On the other hand, he believes that the will of God calls for untiring efforts to work toward a society that lives in conformity to the will of God. Political power and all other efforts are to be used to realize a just social order. Rahman is critical of Christianity because he believes it never envisions any social order.[162]

There is no consensus within the Christian community in regard to the relationship between the gospel and social-political structures. There have been Christians who, like Muslims, have seen the Christian community as God's instrument for ordering society in Jesus' name. John Calvin would represent a moderate example of that understanding. There have been other Christians whose discipleship to the Cosmic Crucified has led them to renounce any use of force to impose God's will on the community. The Lutheran tradition, with its understanding of God's two-kingdom operation, normally attempts to take Jesus' own nonviolent ministry as normative for certain dimensions of life but not all of life. This debate continues within the Christian community even while we become more fully engaged with the Muslim world, which also is being challenged to rethink its traditional understanding of *Sharia* within new contexts.

Christians and Muslims are being forced to think together on this extremely difficult but essential topic because our common human future depends upon it. In some parts of the world, as in Nigeria, we must share our common concerns for life or we will share mutual annihilation.

As Christians enter this dialogue, they will recognize that they are to be conformed to that one who in love was willing to be vulnerable even unto death. Discipleship to the Cosmic Crucified within the Muslim world is an awesome and humbling privilege and task

Chapter 7

The Unique Theological Task in Engaging with Buddhist Peoples

Participation in the mission of the crucified Jesus within a Theravada Buddhist community confronts the Christian witnessing community with a unique and fascinating challenge. It is unique in that Theravada Buddhism articulates a religious view of life without reference to the reality of God. It is fascinating in that its view of life and values are in some ways similar to those reflected in Jesus' life and preaching.

Theravada Buddhism sees cosmic life as a pulsating totality of interdependent experiences and events. Persons, for example, are a confluence of what are termed the five aggregates (collections of substances, sensations, perceptions, volitional activities, and awarenesses), which are in continual flux. The primary presupposition is that underlying this flow of experiences and events experienced as "self or selves" there is no substantive ego or eternal soul. In a similar way there is no ultimate soul/substance that underlies "the cosmic independent fluctuating totality." Furthermore, all metaphysical questions concerning the finitude or infinitude of the totality or even the existence or nonexistence of the Enlightened One after death are metaphysical speculations that have no value in seeking the enlightened path of the Buddha.

In the world of Theravada, philosophical Buddhism, or Zen Buddhism, the Christian encounters persons for whom God is not real or relevant for salvation. That presents an intriguing challenge because the Christian community is forced to reexamine its primary presupposition and make an apology for the reality of God, which is the foundation of the faith.

This challenge is so attractive and disturbing because the values of compassion, love, integrity, and nonviolence espoused by the Buddha are similar to the values embodied and articulated by Jesus of Nazareth. Furthermore, these values are espoused within a philosophy of life that views the world similarly to the Christian perspective.

The Buddha saw life primarily as suffering/ *dukkha*). The world is marked by pain, loss, and impermanence. There are times of love, joy, peace, and happiness; however, they are never permanent and therefore are followed by loss and grief. Suffering or *dukkha* is a mark of life, and enlightened analysis sees that suffering is caused by "selfish" desiring, craving, thirsting. On one level this is reflected in the human desire to live at the expense of the suffering of other persons. On a deeper level suffering is caused by all desire, whether it be selfish, altruistic, or idealistic, for all desire is that dimension of human experience which, because it seeks consequences, continues to imprison life within suffering. However, desire can be eliminated; therefore liberation from suffering is possible. One can eliminate *dukkha* in the realization of *nirvana*, the still point where thirsting and suffering cease.

This analysis reflects motifs similar to the Christian understanding of sin and sin's consequences. Sin is often defined as centering one's life in self or the collective self, rather than in God revealed in Jesus. Lives centered in self or anything less than the God of love result in sin-filled consequences, which result in life filled with pain and suffering. Even though Christians and Buddhists find release from suffering in different ways, they both recognize that suffering is integrally related to a person's primary relationship with God or ultimate reality. Both are also powerful advocates of compassion within the suffering of life. From the Christian perspective, the crucified Jesus places God in the middle of suffering and sees God in Jesus participating in a passionate and compassionate struggle to bring life into the midst of death.

Truth as Walk/Path or Truth as Gift (Grace)

A Buddhist scholar who had devoted several years of study to Christian theology was asked: "What have you found that most clearly distinguishes Buddhist and Christian approaches to truth?" He replied, "In Buddhism everything depends upon myself or us, while in Christianity everything depends upon God or upon grace." The Buddha is reported to have said, "One is one's own refuge, who else could be the refuge?"[163] The Buddha is understood to be the first person of our age to have discovered the way to liberation/ release from suffering, but each one must walk the path alone.

This focus upon human responsibility for walking the way of liberation is fundamental within Theravada Buddhism. It is also a necessity because the human community is not accompanied by God as the Cosmic Companion. For Theravada Buddhism, God is either nonexistent or irrelevant in matters of salvation.

Within this Buddhist context, the message of God's grace— namely, that God in Christ shares the suffering of the human community, becomes vulnerable to death for the human community, and conquers death to transform the broken community and the cosmos—is heard as the consequence of psychological projections or illusions. These Christian beliefs are "strange" but understandable attempts to find peace and security in the fantasies of the human mind rather than facing the reality that we are responsible for walking our own path to liberation or *nirvana.*

There is this remarkable distinction between truth as *walk* and truth as *gift.*

It should be observed that later developments within Mahayana Buddhism spoke of *bodhisattvas* who forfeited for themselves entrance to *nirvana* in order to bring deliverance to suffering people. This particular movement toward grace reached its climax in Japan in a "Pure Land" form of Buddhism taught by Shinran (1173-1262).

Paul Martinson describes this development:

For Shinran human depravity and lostness in ignorance, craving, and self was so deep and sustained that no self-effort leading to salvation was possible. The only hope was for an act of grace that came from the outside. This act was the ancient vow (promise) of the Amida Buddha eons ago that he not attain enlightenment unless all other beings also be guaranteed enlightenment thereby. That guarantee was to be theirs with only the simple calling on his name.[164]

Zen Buddhism, another form of Mahayana Buddhism developed in Japan, reflects the original Buddhist vision of finding refuge in oneself. A popular quote from Zen illustrates this fact. "If you meet the Buddha on the road, kill him." Here once again one confronts the distinction between truth as walk/path and truth as gift.

Daisetz Teitaro Suzuki, the Japanese Zen scholar, writes: "For whatever authority there is in Zen, all comes from within."[165]

The Reality of the Totality or God and Creation

A Buddhist-Christian seminar on religion and suffering was held in Chicago in December 1991. One of the sessions dealt with Christian and Buddhist involvement in development work. A Christian, in addressing this topic, used the term "creation." A Buddhist scholar immediately raised his hand to speak and then stated that the term "creation" implied a Christian faith statement concerning the Creator. Because the Buddhists at the table did not see reality in those dualistic terms, he requested that a neutral term such as "nature" or "natural environment" be used in the discussion of development. In a later discussion, centered upon Christian chaplaincy work within hospitals, a Lutheran pastor spoke of sharing the love of God with the sick and dying. Once again a Buddhist participant's hand went up. He stated that his Buddhist students often asked, "Why do Christians find it necessary to state that God loves them when they are surrounded by the love of people?" These Theravada Buddhist questions indicate a second difference between the Buddhist and Christian visions of reality. For Christians, God is encountered as the Other, the awesome Wholly Other, who in costly love is passionately involved in human existence. For Buddhism, God as the encountered Wholly Other is nonexistent or irrelevant to salvation.

Walpola Sri Rahula, the Theravada Buddhist scholar, writes:

According to Buddhism, our ideas of God and Soul are false and empty. Though highly developed as theories, they are all the same extremely subtle mental projections, garbed in an intricate metaphysical and philosophical phraseology.[166]

The denial of God and soul is grounded in the Buddhist vision of reality as the sum total of all events and relationships behind which there are no eternal entities or identities. Behind the sum of the five aggregates (matter, sensations, perceptions, mental formations, consciousness) which are experienced as "myself" there is no permanent, eternal "Soul" or "Ego."[167] My experienced self is simply the fusion of those five aggregates at this particular present time. In the same way there is no permanent Cosmic-Self (God-Atman) behind the flux of the sum total of all reality.

Christians and other theists have often argued that everything must have a cause, and there must then be a First Cause, God. But when Christians are asked, "Where then does God come from?" the answer is simply, God is the Uncaused Mysterious Cause behind life who needs no cause. The Buddhist replies, if logically God can be an uncaused mystery, why cannot the "sum total of all reality" be an uncaused mystery. Like the presumed God, it is simply "there." Whether this Uncaused Reality is eternal or not eternal, finite or infinite, are speculative questions of no relevance for the path of liberation/deliverance which results in *nirvana*.[168]

Christian-Muslim discussions center in the nature of God. Discussions with Theravada Buddhists center in the reality of God. Why as Christians do we speak of God? What can we say to the Theravada Buddhist concerning the grounds of our vision, our conviction that we as the human community are accompanied by the awesome Cosmic Companion, God!

Traditionally, Christian theists have argued for the existence of God by arguing from cause to the First Cause; from contingency to Ultimate Necessity; from design to the Designer; from the claim of values or the sense of "ought" to the One who makes those claims or commands the ought; from the giftedness of existence to the Giver of existence.[169]

The Buddhist may respond that causal relationships simply "are" and need no First Cause any more than God necessitates the creator of God. Contingency simply is and needs no Ultimate Necessity, or contingency is the Ultimate necessity. Design is simply a mark of the cosmic totality, which is a given mystery of design much the same way that God is concluded by the theists to be the given Designer Mystery. And values are simply recognized as good and need no ground in the Value Giver. When the Christian argues that life is experienced as a given, implying a Giver, the Buddhist may reply that life as the sum total of reality is itself the giftedness requiring no Giver. However, the Buddhist may reply that life is not giftedness at all because life is ultimately marked by suffering, which is the given from which one seeks release.

In this manner, the Buddhist may reject the traditional arguments for God as logically not necessary. However, in response the Christian theist may see in them testimony to the reality of God. They may appear as evidence much in the same way as circumstantial evidence is brought into a courtroom. They are not logically conclusive proof, but they may be seen by the Christian theist as signs of the reality of God. The givenness and giftedness of life are testimony pointing to the Giver of life. The design and meaningfulness of existence are testimony pointing to the Designer of life. The contingency of life points to that lying behind contingency, the Ultimate Necessity. In summary, in the experiences of giftedness, meaning and contingency, faith sees the Giver, the Designer, the Ultimate Necessity, God. It should be noted that there are a few persons continuing to call themselves Christians who have rejected theism and view reality in the unitary sense found in the Buddhist vision. For them God designates the dimension of reality that is experienced as the awesome givenness, meaning and mystery of it all.

Having shared this metaphysical debate, the Christian must state that the biblical faith did not arise out of a theological conversation or dialogue. Rather, the biblical and apostolic faith arose out of a faith encounter with God. In the voice of the prophets, the people of Israel with "ears to hear" heard and encountered the speaking God. In the events of Israel's history, such as the Exodus and the destruction of Jerusalem, those who had "eyes to see" saw the action of God. In the life, death and resurrection of Jesus, the "eyes of faith" saw and encountered the presence, the voice and activity of God. In Israel's and the church's worshipful (Psalms), reasonable (Wisdom, Epistles), missionary (Prophets, Epistles) response to God, the "eyes and ears" of faith encountered God. God was that awesome, gracious, disturbing Reality that called, empowered, comforted, challenged, and led a people who had "eyes to see and ears to hear." God called through an inner voice or in the words of a fellow human (prophet). God in and through events saved (Exodus), judged (fall of Jerusalem) and challenged (rebuild Jerusalem's walls). In the Jesus crucified, God called, forgave, challenged, empowered, comforted, saved. In and through the experiences of life, the "eyes and ears" of faith encountered the living God.

It was this experience of the encountered One, that One who stood over against the human community, that was ultimately the grounds for speaking of God. Abraham, Moses, Isaiah, Jeremiah, Jesus, Peter, Paul, and all persons of faith have encountered that gracious and disturbing Reality who unsettled their lives, made them restless with their own souls and their communities, and who ultimately gave them meaning and security within the brokenness and suffering of human existence. People of faith point to this divine-human encounter as the ground of talk of God.[170]

The most powerful testimony of God's over-againstness of reality is faith's encounter with Jesus' resurrection from the dead. Death is the universal mark of human and biological existence. Death seems inevitably to follow life. The resurrection runs counter to that universal order and as such is testimony to God as that reality who is encountered in the midst of life in Jesus Christ.[171]

The Buddhist may readily account for these experiences as psychological constructs interpreting natural human experiences or simply illusions of human communities who find it impossible to face the reality of human suffering or to take responsibility for one's own deliverance.

As Christians who have the privilege of seeing and hearing God in and through the flow of human existence, we live in amazing gratitude for the eyes that see and the ears that hear. The questions of possible illusions are not met by counter charges of blindness and rebellion. Rather, they are met by the challenge to witness to the presence and action of God within the human family, the life of Israel, and the incarnate Cosmic Crucified in order that others, in faith, may encounter that God who is passionately involved in their lives and who in concretized form went through hell for their own sake.

Dukkha (Suffering) or Sin and Its Consequences

Christianity and Buddhism perceive existence in similar terms. Both understand existence other than one would desire or hope it to be. The Buddha's teaching centers in the Four Noble Truths:

1. *Dukkha*
2. The arising/origin of *dukkha*
3. The cessation of *dukkha*
4. The way leading to the cessation of *dukkha*[172]

The Four Noble Truths revolve around *dukkha*, a Pali word meaning suffering, pain, sorrow, misery, in contrast to happiness. Buddhist scholars note that the word has deeper connotations within a religious discussion, such as imperfection, impermanence, and emptiness. According to Walpola Rahula, the word "realistically" designates life as it is and is the point from which one longs for that which is hoped and desired: freedom, peace, tranquility.

This does not mean that the Buddhist does not recognize experiences of happiness such as family happiness, friendship happiness, aesthetic pleasure; however, these experiences of happiness are not permanent. They come and go, and with their passing comes a sense of sadness and loss. Furthermore, life is marked by many types of pain, both mental and physical, such as disease, death, poverty, loneliness and conflict caused by greed, hate, tyranny, etc. Buddhism basically sees life characterized by *dukkha* as that from which the thoughtful person will seek liberation or deliverance.

In a somewhat similar manner, Christianity views life as marked by suffering and brokenness. Life is marked by estrangement, alienation, loneliness, strife, conflict, lovelessness, meaninglessness. From the Christian perspective, life is not as God intends it to be, as it was, as it ought to be, nor as it will be! Christian thought understands this suffering and brokenness to be rooted in sin and its consequences.

Sin is described as a state of being in which God and God's will are not accepted as the center/basis for life. Humanity, rather than centering in God, trusting God, obeying God, is determined to center in (trust in or obey) something less than God, whether it be nation, family or the individual self. This primal stance with or against the God who is compassionately and creatively involved in life has consequences for every dimension of life.[173]

For example, trust and obedience in God (centering in God) who has created and loves the whole human family and who intends the human family to live in love and trust of each other means that humanity will be called and empowered to love and trust each other. Centering in God will mean centering in God's human family. Turning from God in distrust (unfaith) and disobedience will mean a breach in the God-human relationship, but it will also result in broken relationships between persons. This interdependency of relationships is seen in the creation-fall accounts in Genesis 1-2. When Adam and Eve break their relationship with God, they are estranged from each other. They make themselves clothing, signifying their estrangement, and Adam blames his fallen state upon Eve, who had been given to him as God's intended companion (a state of alienation).

One can similarly note that in moving from being God-centered (faith) to other than God-centered, humanity moves from innocence to guilt; from living relationships to alienation; from trusting responsibility to God and God's children to irresponsibility; from *shalom* to destructive conflict, from creative servanthood to exploitive domination; and from life to death. Life is broken; suffering and pain are essential marks of human existence. In biblical terms, people long for their liberation, their deliverance, their redemption.

This realistic perspective on the tragedy of human existence is shared by Buddhists and Christians. We have a very different vision of humanity's ultimate liberation; however, we do share common convictions concerning the necessity of our compassionate involvement with people on behalf of a common struggle for justice and peace within the tragedies of life.

Buddhist Denial of the Ego or Christian Self-Denial

Christian discipleship is Jesus' call to "deny themselves and take up their cross and follow me. For those who want to save their life will lose it, and those who lose their life for my sake, and for the sake of the gospel, will save it" (Mk 8:34-35). Jesus calls his disciples to deny themselves—to say no to themselves—in order that they may say yes to God in the Cosmic Crucified. In our earlier discussion dealing with being conformed to Jesus Christ, we noted that in Paul and Luther there is the declaration that the "old" self which does not wish to be conformed to God's will must die in order that the "new" self wishing to be conformed to God's will might rise or come to life.

Christian self-denial is a surrender to God and God's will. It is surrender to the God-in-Christ-centered life in order to become a Cosmic Crucified-centered life. Christian self-denial has at times deteriorated into an attitude in which one despises oneself. Within early Christianity, influenced by Gnosticism, which elevated spirit and despised matter, people became disgusted with their existence as flesh and blood. The flesh was to be despised and neglected as one, for example, lived in filth or one remained celibate, being uninvolved in the fleshly things of life. Within medieval Christianity with its focus upon guilt and the terror of judgment, one, in self-denial, tormented the sinful self through disciplines of fasting or self-flagellation in order to purify the soul. These examples of self-denial are distortions of Jesus' call to discipleship, to conformity with Christ.

Christian self-denial is the call of the Cosmic Crucified to say no to self, to anything less than God, in order to say yes with one's whole being to God. Protestant theology has emphasized that human pride is often that which stands in the way of self-surrender to God. Human pride must die that Christ might be Lord of life.[174] Contemporary forms of liberation theology have noted that persons may not only see themselves as "more than" God intends them to be (pride) but they may see themselves as "less than" God intends them to be (self-effacement). Persons may deny their God-given value and giftedness.

In this case, self-denial means saying no to one's denial of one's own value and giftedness in order that one can say yes to God's call to serve Jesus Christ with one's God-given gifts.

The Buddhist also speaks of denying the self, but in totally different terms. When Buddhism speaks of the non-substantiality of the ego or the doctrine of the No-Soul (*Anatta*), it does not speak in terms of a spiritual and moral encounter with God, but rather speaks of a metaphysical fact.[175] Buddhism begins with an analysis of the self and comes to the conclusion that the self is a confluence of the five aggregates underlying which there is no lasting entity that can be designated the self or the soul.

Christian self-denial is a surrender of one's life to the mission of God that sweeps one into the world in order that one might participate in God's mission to transform the totality of reality. Buddhist denial of the self is a recognition of the metaphysical insight that the self is ultimately a transient reality, which makes release from the cycle of suffering (*samsara*) possible.

Nirvana or Resurrection and a New Creation

For the Buddhist, *nirvana* is liberation, deliverance from *dukkha* and is the awakening enlightenment. The Four Noble Truths again are:

1. *Dukkha*
2. The arising/origin of *dukkha*
3. The cessation of *dukkha*
4. The way leading to the cessation of *dukkha* -*Nirvana*

Buddhism must be seen on the background of Hinduism, which envisions existence as a continual cycle of existence, including incarnations and reincarnations of the soul. This cycle of existence (*samsara*) is experienced as that from which one desires deliverance. Within this cyclical existence, the law of *karma* is at work, rewarding good and punishing evil. Living contrary to that which is good produces punishing consequences in future incarnations and vice versa. Ultimate deliverance within Hinduism occurs when the individual soul (*atman*) is recognized and experienced as one with the Cosmic Soul (*Atman*).

Buddhism assumes that existence is cyclical and *karma* is at work through experiences of reincarnation; however, as noted earlier, it rejects the reality of a permanent *atman* (soul) or *Atman* (God). Within this context, Buddhism begins with *dukkha* (the First Noble Truth).

This is followed by the Second Noble Truth which states that *dukkha* arises from thirst, craving, desire (*tanha*):

It is this "thirst," which produces re-existence and re-becoming, and which is bound up with passionate greed, and which finds fresh delight now here and now there, namely, (1) thirst for sense pleasure, (2) thirst for existence and becoming and (3) thirst for non-existence.[176]

Thirst in the sense of greed often causes suffering for the exploited and also for the greedy. Thirst in the form of sensual desire causes the suffering of exploitation and abuse within sexual relationships. It must be noted, however, that Buddhism understands thirst in a much deeper and more comprehensive manner. Any desire to exist, to continue within the realm of *dukkha*, participates in and prolongs the unsatisfactoriness of existence. A thirst for that which is beautiful or good also extends this existence. Paradoxically, even the thirst for nonexistence prevents one's awakening, the realization of *nirvana*. *Nirvana* is when thirst of any kind ceases.[177]

Nirvana may be realized in this life, or it may be realized in some future reincarnation, or in some "heavenly" dimension of existence. The famous Thai Buddhist monk Buddhadasa interestingly argues that enlightenment or the attainment of *nirvana* is more readily attained within the human state.

The expression "happy state (*nirvana*) in the human realm" signifies that in the human realm impermanence, unsatisfactoriness, and non-selfhood can more readily be perceived than in the celestial realm. In the human realm there are enlightened beings, there are *arahants* [enlightened ones], and there are the Buddha, Dhamma [teaching], and Sangha [the community]. In the celestial realm, that jungle of sensuality, there are none of these things. Thus, celestial beings come to the human realm in search of the happy state...Some people seek paradise, happiness in the next existence, in the realm of celestial beings. They invest in it by making merit, giving to charity, selling their houses and goods, and building things in monasteries. Where is the genuinely happy state to be found? Think it over.[178]

Buddhadasa makes it clear that *nirvana* is attainable here and now. *Nirvana* "is to be found in dying before death."[179] One should note that Buddhadasa is not always popular among many traditional Thai Buddhist monks.

When *nirvana* is realized, the forces which produced *dukkha*, the cyclical realm of suffering, cease because there is no more thirst for continuing existence. There is now a "still-point"; the cycle of suffering is followed by a indescribable and incomprehensible awakening that must be experienced to be known—*nirvana*.

Walpola Rahula in pointing to *nirvana* quotes several Pali texts:

> He who has realized the Truth, *Nirvana*, is the happiest being in the world. He is free from all "complexes" and obsessions, the worries and troubles that torment others. His mental health is perfect. He does not repent the past, nor does he brood over the future. He lives fully in the present. Therefore he appreciates and enjoys things in the purest sense without self-projections. He is joyful, exultant, enjoying the pure life, his faculties pleased, free from anxiety, serene and peaceful. As he is free from selfish desire, hatred, ignorance, conceit, pride, and all such "defilements," he is pure and gentle, full of universal love, compassion, kindness, sympathy, understanding and tolerance. His service to others is of the purest, for he has no thought of self. He gains nothing, accumulates nothing, not even anything spiritual, because he is free from the illusion of Self, and the "thirst" for becoming.[180]

Christianity views deliverance (salvation) very differently. In contrast to the unitary view of existence envisioned by Buddhism, Christians believe that they have encountered God. God who is concretized in Jesus the crucified is the Cosmic Companion who accompanies the human community through the suffering of existence. God disturbs and unsettles our lives calling humanity to repentance and cruciform discipleship as God transforms the totality of creation. The Cosmic Companion concretized in Jesus was vulnerable to death in order that humanity might be forgiven and reconciled to the Father/Mother of life; God as Cosmic Liberator conquers death and leads God's people into resurrection life.

In encountering God within creation and history, Christians trust that all of life is rooted in God's creative and gracious action. God's passionate concern for life, for people, righteousness and justice indicate that all of life is from God; it is God's good creation. God's incarnation in the flesh and blood of Jesus is indicative that all of life (physical, psychological, spiritual) is of God and ultimately a created gift of God. The resurrection of Jesus Christ, rather than spiritual or psychic appearances of Jesus, is testimony that God ultimately is committed to the transformation of a concrete world where "all God's children got shoes" and live in the illuminating presence of the God who dwells with God's people.

Participation in this God-created cosmic reality, the resurrection life, is by invitation of Jesus the Cosmic Crucified. Like the grace of forgiveness, it is sheer gift. It is rooted in the resurrection of Jesus Christ[181] and is promised to those who are incorporated into his life and mission.

> Death has been swallowed up in victory.
>
> Where, O death, is your victory?
>
> Where, O death, is your sting?"
>
> The sting of death is sin, and the power of sin is the law. But thanks be to God, who gives us the victory through our Lord Jesus Christ.
>
> Therefore, my beloved, be steadfast, immovable, always excelling in the work of the Lord, because you know that in the Lord your labor is not in vain. (1 Cor 15:54-58)

A question is always raised within the context of this resurrection promise. Are only Christians given this promise? I still remember African students asking about the eternal destiny of parents or grandparents who had died before the preaching of the gospel.

The Christian celebration of the resurrection faith is not to be mistaken for the assertion that the eternal destiny of every person depends upon meeting this Jesus through the preaching of the gospel within history or being recognized members of our Christian institutions.

There are passages within the Bible which state that to meet Jesus Christ is to have confronted judgment and life:

> Indeed, God did not send the Son into the world to condemn the world, but in order that the world might be saved through him. [Those] who believe in him are not condemned; but [those] who [do] not believe are condemned already,...this is the judgment, that the light has come into the world, and people loved darkness rather than light because their deeds are evil. (John 3:17-21)

This and similar passages make it clear that a positive or negative response to encountering God's light in Jesus has present and eternal consequences. The Johannine passage, similar to many other biblical texts, makes assertions about those who have had the privilege of meeting authentic light in Jesus. Those who have met Jesus and trusted the light met in Jesus have already passed from darkness into light, from death to life. They already dwell within the incredible reality of God's light concretized in Jesus, the magnificence of the messianic reign of God in Christ. In the words of Romans 10:13-17, they have called upon the name of the Lord and have been saved.

John 3:17-21 and similar texts also indicate that those who have met Jesus and rejected God's truth concretized in Jesus have already been judged as outside the messianic kingdom because they loved the darkness rather than the light. This text and similar texts do not make any statement about those who have not met the truth or seen the light in Jesus. They have not yet been through judgment. One can also state that there are many who have never met the truth and light of Jesus even though they have heard of Jesus. We as Christians have so distorted Jesus the Christ that we have made it impossible for grace and truth (John 1:14) in Jesus to be known and experienced by those that we have oppressed and crushed or by those who cannot see Jesus in the entanglements of our theological or confessional statements. The contemporary Jewish community would certainly be one example.

In evangelical circles questions are always raised as to how God will ultimately deal with those who have never heard or who have misheard the gospel. One simply trusts that they are in the hands of the God concretized in Jesus Crucified, knowing that the same compassion, grace, and forgiveness embrace all of us. Their salvation, like ours, is grounded in the love of God, the pain-love and suffering of God.

Many biblical passages indicate that the culminating feast and banquet will be much more inclusive than some Christians might expect. Jesus, having heard the words of a Roman centurion, said, "Truly I tell you, in no one in Israel have I found such faith. I tell you, many will come from east and west and will eat with Abraham and Isaac and Jacob in the kingdom of heaven, while the heirs of the kingdom will be thrown into the outer darkness" (Mt 8:10-11). In Luke 10, Jesus portrays life within the kingdom of God in the person of a heretical Samaritan. In Luke 18:9-14, an unknown sinner cries out for grace and unknowingly returns home justified before God. In John, Jesus states, "I have other sheep that do not belong to this fold. I must bring them also, and they will listen to my voice" (John 10:16).

Paul, speaking to Athenians, stated there are times of ignorance that God overlooks, not calling persons to accountability before Christ (Acts 17:30). In Romans 2 Paul writes that all humanity has the law of God written on their hearts which "will accuse or perhaps excuse them on the day when, according to my gospel, God, through Jesus Christ, will judge the secret thoughts of all" (Rom 2:15-16). Ephesians 1 speaks of a divine plan to gather all things in him, things in heaven and things on earth (Eph 1:9-10). The Apostle Peter writes of a mission of Christ to the realm of the imprisoned dead who had been disobedient in the times of Noah (1 Pt 3:18-20). In these passages there are enough inspired glimpses of the new heaven and new earth to indicate that God's future messianic banquet will shatter and transcend our anticipations!

The Path Leading to the Cessation of *Dukkha* and the Way of the Cross

For the Christian, the way of the cross is primarily the Cosmic Crucified's way in the world; therefore, the way of the cross is God's way and God's walk through a broken and suffering world. Only secondarily is it our way in the world as God in Christ calls, renews and empowers us to be conformed to the Cosmic Crucified. In conformity to Christ, we are called and empowered to compassionate self-giving service, to vulnerability in mission, to a continuing struggle for peace, justice and wholeness of life.

The way or path within Theravada Buddhism is "my" path. As the young Buddhist said, "for Christians all depends upon God and God's grace, for Buddhists all depends upon us." Few Christians, however, would challenge the values called for by the Fourth Noble Truths (The Path):

1. Right Understanding
2. Right Thought
3. Right Speech
4. Right Action
5. Right Livelihood
6. Right Effort
7. Right Mindfulness
8. Right Concentration

The path is devoted to ethical conduct, to mental discipline and wisdom. Walpola Rahula writes: "Ethical Conduct is built on the vast conception of universal love and compassion for all living beings, on which the Buddha's teaching is based."[182] He further states "that compassion represents love, charity, kindness, tolerance and such noble qualities on the emotional side, or qualities of the heart." The Buddhist Path also includes qualities of the mind including mental discipline and wisdom.

The Buddhist understanding of the qualities of the heart, including love, compassion, charity and kindness, are strikingly similar to the values called for in Jesus' preaching and teaching. Christians immediately think of Jesus' parable of the Good Samaritan or Jesus' saying, "Love your neighbor as yourself" (Mt 19:19). Buddhists think of Buddha's sayings:

> One should win anger through kindness, wickedness through goodness, selfishness through charity and falsehood through truthfulness.[183]

However, that which is most nearly identical is the advocacy for non-violence by both Buddha and Jesus. Wapola Rahula writes:

> It is too well known to be repeated here that Buddhism advocates and preaches non-violence and peace as its universal message, and does not approve of any kind of violence or destruction of life. According to Buddhism there is nothing that can be called a "just war"—which is only a false term coined and put into circulation to justify and excuse hatred, cruelty, violence and massacre. Who decides what is just or unjust? The mighty and the victorious are "just," and the weak and the defeated are "unjust." Our war is always "just," and your war is always "unjust." Buddhism does not accept this position.[184]

The common emphasis upon compassion, love, kindness, non-violence has on many occasions attracted Buddhists and Christians to each other. The Buddha has been an attractive figure for some Christians, and Jesus has been an attractive figure for some Buddhists.

The Buddhist Path includes qualities of the mind as well as qualities of the heart. They are both included within the same walk. One does not progress from one to the other; both are essential to the walk along which enlightenment may take place. In order to develop qualities of the mind, Buddhism emphasizes meditation, and meditation may be defined as mental development. There are two forms of meditation.

The first is the development of mental concentration. Various methods are used to focus the mind, leading to mystic states. Buddhism, however, does not regard the mystic states as "enlightenment." They are mind created or induced and have nothing to do with reality - *nirvana*. There, then, is a second form of meditation which is insight into the nature of things. This is insight into *dukkha*, the rise of *dukkha*, the cessation of *dukkha* leading to wisdom and "the complete liberation of the mind, to the realization of Ultimate Truth, *Nirvana*."[185]

Some Christians have been deeply impressed with the value of Buddhist meditation, the mental discipline and its healing effects upon the human personality. I would not question the value of this mental discipline. I believe that the Western activist mentality can learn from meditative disciplines of the East. Persons need time to stop and center one's being. However, ultimately Christian meditation will be different from Buddhist meditation in that one either perceives reality as Self-Walk or as an accompanied journey with the Cosmic Companion. Enlightenment comes when the walk ceases and the "still-point" is realized. God's walk, which passionately embraces creation and humanity, is realized in a new creation when all tears are wiped away and death, mourning, crying and pain will be no more for the first things have passed away (Rev 21:4).

These very different perspectives draw persons in different cosmic directions. The Buddhist perspective draws persons out of the cyclical, transient realm of *dukkha*. It draws them out of attachment to the cycle of suffering in order to realize that still-point where *dukkha* ceases. The Cosmic Crucified calls humanity into the pain and suffering in order that life and creation might be transformed as a new creation. As Buddhists and Christians are drawn in these different cosmic directions, they will often find that they share common visions and struggles for the alleviation of pain in the middle of life. Compassion and non-violence are marks of the Way of the Buddha as well as the Way of the Cross!

Chapter 8

A Radical Call
to a Radical Witness

Jesus and the cross concretize the radical gift of God's Kingdom. At the heart of that gift is Jesus' embodiment of a creative, life-affirming and transforming vulnerable love which embraces not only the world but the universe. Every galaxy, every child, every creature, every electron, move within the compassion of God who "weeps" in the midst of suffering and "sings" in the midst of creation's joys. Most miraculously, God's ultimate gift of love is not God's irresistible omnipotence, but God's vulnerable movement of "pain-love" into our lives. Only love that is willing to share human suffering and bear with human faithlessness and rebellion is capable of sharing transforming grace and forgiveness with us. Only Divine vulnerable love which does not crush our resistance but persuasively draws us out of brokenness and overwhelms us with grace and forgiveness is capable of transforming our lives. Compassion, grace, forgiveness and trust emerge from an encounter with compassion, grace, forgiveness and trust. Only vulnerable love authentically transforms life. Ultimate truth is crucified truth. Jesus as crucified truth calls us into participation in crucified truth.

Witnessing That Humanity May Trust and Hope

We trust that this knowing of God in Jesus crucified is radically good news—Gospel! It is such good news that it might appear to be unbelievable in a world marked by brokenness, suffering and pain. In a world of suffering is it possible that God is Love (1 John 4:8)? Persons have always asked, "Can this possibly be true?" "Can the news be this good?" I have often said "I can understand why people in a world of suffering and absurdity are agnostics or atheists; however, I cannot understand why people who believe in Jesus as the crucified truth do not want to speak about the gospel, share this good news in order that others might trust in it.

I do, however, understand that the church has often so distorted Jesus as the crucified that there are those who refuse to be identified with the distortion. People are ashamed when the name of Jesus is used to fight wars, whether military, religious, political or ecclesiastical; exploit the marginalized, whether they are people of color, women, gays and lesbians or those afflicted with AIDS; or ridicule the faith of Buddhists, Hindus, or Muslims. One must add that when the distortions are so grotesque that the crucified truth is lost, then it is time for the church, in Jesus' name, to remain silent and take time to reevaluate its understanding of the crucified truth.[186]

The mission of the church must recapture the name of the Jesus of the New Testament. For it is through this Jesus crucified that one sees and knows the heart of God. There is no other revelation that knows God in this distinct and incomprehensible way. Nowhere else does one encounter God, who has shared the depths of brokenness and the hell of betrayal in order that we may have life. We witness to Jesus as the Word of God in order that persons may trust in this Good News and walk in this vision and this light.

A number of years ago an Evangelical Lutheran Church in America missionary working in West Africa asked, "Frankly, I guess what I want to know is whether you want us to make disciples of Muslim peoples?" I wrote in response:

> I have indicated that our work is rooted in the finality of Jesus. There is no hidden or revealed God other than the suffering God concretized in the abandoned and crucified one. For the Christian that is ultimate truth and ultimate grace; therefore, it will be shared. It is to be shared not because the crucified one with imperial power threatens to crush or torment in eternity those who have not heard or believed, but because this incredible treasure of truth and grace should be shared with every person within the human community! Jesus insists that all are to share in the reality of God's kingdom embodied in Jesus: "Go...and make disciples of all nations,..." (Matt. 28:19). For the sake of every person who is destined to walk this planet, the treasure is not to be hidden! It is to be proclaimed that God is ultimately compassion and grace and embraces in love the whole human community. It is to be shared that every broken and lonely individual so often lost within the wilderness of crowds and masses is passionately known and loved by God. It is to be announced and

known that whenever one broken soul in despair cries for forgiveness and hope in the night, that she or he, knowingly or not, is already forgiven and at peace with God, whose embrace has taken the form of arms with nail-pierced hands. In Jesus' name, it is to be announced to those whose self-esteem has been crushed by religious and cultural oppression that they, too, have been created in the image of God and have gifts and potential yet undreamed of. It must be proclaimed to those who understand every tragedy and every tear as the consequence of God's hidden and capricious will, that God, although hidden, is absolutely and ultimately *for* them. It is to be announced to those who despair when compassion and justice are crushed and life is consumed by death that Jesus is raised as the first fruits of God's re-creation. Life will spring forth from death! This is the treasure that births and nurtures trust and hope.

God's call to repentance voiced and embodied in Jesus as prophet must also be universally announced. The prophetic voice of Jesus must be allowed to challenge every person, group, society, organization and nation. Every person and every human structure in some way embodies the demonic principalities and powers that dehumanize the whole of creation and its peoples. Jesus as raised prophet spoke not only to ancient Galilean crowds but speaks to the teeming masses that inhabit the 250 nations claiming autonomy at the beginning of the 21st century. Wherever people and life are crushed, wherever love is absent, justice perverted, the good betrayed and the beautiful disgraced, there the risen prophet must be enabled to speak. God's voice must be heard, 'Repent, for the kingdom of God is at hand.' People are to be challenged to repentance in Jesus' name. For the sake of their own life and for the sake of the lives they ignore and destroy, they are called to repentance.

To those who in repentance know themselves as broken, Jesus promises, 'Your sins are forgiven; go in peace.' To those who trust him, Jesus is heard to say, 'Take up your cross and follow me!'

My missionary friend still asks "But do you want us to make disciples out of Muslim people?" If you mean do you want the hearts and minds of our Muslim friends to be molded by God as embodied in Jesus then I desire that they be followers of Jesus! If you mean do you want Muslim people to find faith, hope, and love in God's incredible prophetic embodiment in Jesus, then I desire that they trust and live within this truth. I also pray that they may possibly find that vision of reality within our Christian Church. However, if you mean do I insist that life and salvation can only be found in Christian confession or in *membership* in our Christian churches, then I know that the God identified in Jesus is not locked up in a Christian, Jewish, Muslim or Buddhist box, and I know that the traditional social structures of Islamic society, the historical tensions existing between our communities and the brokenness of our own Christian churches normally makes that an impossibility. It may mean that God intends to work out God's own future for Christians and Muslims in terms that we have not dreamed of. (It could be that Jesus might be received as the crucified Word of God within the Muslim community in ways unknown and unexpected by us.)

Finally, as Christians who wish to share the cruciform message and mission of Jesus, and also as Christians who recognize the depths of our own brokenness and the brokenness of all humanity, we pray that we might at least fragmentarily be true and faithful in our witness to God's love and truth spoken and embodied in Jesus. Our claims to truth and faith are not claims of religious or spiritual superiority, nor claims of future privileged positions in eternity. They are confessions of witnesses who believe that they have been captured by an ultimate and unsurpassable vision of universal truth, grace, and life, which God brings into existence through the Messianic mission, crucifixion and resurrection of the risen prophet Jesus. They are confessions of those who trust that the unconditional love embodied in Jesus already grasps all of humanity. The totality of creation lives within the embrace of God concretized in Jesus, the Cosmic Crucified. No human limitations are excluded from that forgiving embrace of God.

The Emergence of Centers of Radical Witness to Crucified Truth

As persons are grasped by the Good News and become disciples, it is empowering for them that they experience the privilege of community within the Jesus movement. The Christian community is gathered (called out) from the human family by the call of Jesus and they are gathered in Jesus' name as the body of Christ (1 Cor. 12). Within this community, Christ is present. "Where two or three are gathered in my name, I am there among them" (Mt 18:20). Christ is present, speaks, and acts as the Word of God when Jesus crucified is preached and taught. This preached and taught Word is made alive within the believers and community through the power of the Holy Spirit. The same Jesus as the Christ is present, speaks, and acts through Baptism and the Lord's Supper. Within the Protestant community, these are the only essential unifying marks of the church. All else may be created to enable the local church to be freely and powerfully a new expression of the body of Christ. The Augsburg Confession, Article VII reads: "For the true unity of the church it is enough to agree concerning the teaching of the gospel and the administration of the sacraments. It is not necessary that human traditions or rites and ceremonies, instituted by men, should be alike everywhere." A statement by Herbert Butterfield (a British theologian) affirms this more powerfully: "Hold to Christ, and for the rest be totally uncommitted."[187]

Within this community (*koinonia*), there is to be: 1) a reconciled human family; 2) healing and nurture for the broken and suffering; and 3) the mandate and empowerment for mission. The visible church is both an actualization and distortion of this God-intended community, the body of Christ.[188]

Insofar as the church manifests the authentic body of Christ, it is a sign of God-given hope in the world.

Centers of Reconciled Community Within Human Alienation

The world is marred by enmity and alienation. Individuals, families, communities and nations distrust, compete, struggle and destroy one another. Human lives and history seem to be a continual narrative of conflict with intervals of peace. The consequences of this global estrangement are incredible suffering and pain. Estranged persons live out their lives in loneliness. Alienated persons consign one another to pain, poverty and oppression. Enmity results in strife, war and the death of millions.

The world hungers for reconciliation and unity. It longs for peace the cessation of hostilities, quiet streets and silent nights. The world dreams of what Scripture describes as a new creation or new heaven and a new earth.

Within this search for unity, the church is called to be a sign of reconciliation and hope. The church is a reconciled community. God was in Christ reconciling the world unto himself and reconciling those at enmity with each other. In Christ there is neither male nor female, slave nor free, Jew nor Gentile. God in Christ has broken down all the walls of separation. In conformity to Jesus the crucified and Prince of Peace, we are called to cross all boundaries in order to share God's embrace of the world.

One of the most impressive symbols of the power of reconciliation is found on walls of churches in the Papua New Guinea highlands. Numerous local spears, hang on the walls on the house of the Prince of Peace. Spears have already been beaten into plowshares. Warring clans and peoples have thrown down their weapons of death and as a reconciled people share a holy banquet of life and peace.

As a church we are called to participate more fully in the unity of the body of Christ as a sign of hope. We are called to be a community in which all the walls of separation are challenged and ultimately destroyed. Racism, sexism, nationalism, denominationalism are all to be challenged in order that the church might be a sign of the eventual unity of the total cosmos. For in Christ all things hold together.

> He has made known to us the mystery of his will, according to his good pleasure that he set forth in Christ as a plan for the fullness of time, to gather up all things in him, things in heaven and things on earth. (Eph 1:9-10)

In Christ, Christians are called to die to our own narrow dreams and visions in order that we might participate more completely in the fullness of the Kingdom of God.

Centers of Healing and Nurture Within Brokenness and Suffering

Believers in Jesus the Christ enter into a new life marked by acceptance and forgiveness. The baptismal waters announce that the past is forgiven; it is buried and cleansed. The believer is given a new identity as a child of God. The child is baptized in Jesus' name (early Christian formulation [Acts 10:48]) or in the name of the Father, Son and Holy Spirit (Mt 28). One belongs to God and has a new family name declaring the intrinsic value of every person created by God and of every person for whom Jesus died. The new believer is, and experiences being, reconciled to God and reconciled within God's family. Within this family there is security, a sense of meaning in mission and a hope that disarms the power of death.

The believers, however, continue to be marked by sin and its consequences. Distrust, self-centeredness, disobedience still pervade life. Life is still broken and marked by pain as alienation, guilt, loneliness, irresponsibility, strife, and all the suffering that results from being enmeshed in a sinful world. Martin Luther speaks of being both sinner and saint, that is, broken and forgiven believer.

Congregations are centers of healing and nurture for broken believers. Christians gather to hear the healing power of the gospel. Forgiveness, comfort, hope, meaning are shared in the reading of Scripture, the preaching of Jesus the Cosmic Crucified, and the celebration of the sacraments. Then there are prayers as the community pours out their gratitude and petitions to God. Prayers are consolation and hope as a people consciously walk and talk with their Cosmic Companion. Then there are hymns of praise; words of encouragement; handclasps and hugs of solidarity as people are fused, healed and empowered by God and God's family.

Healed, nurtured and empowered, the believers leave. They are sent to proclaim that Jesus Christ is Lord and Savior through words and deeds.

The twentieth-century third-world saw an incredible explosion of the Pentecostal/Charismatic movement. The Spirit was experienced in visions, divine guidance, spiritual healings and the exorcism of demons. Prophets arose who led God's people in battles with the demonic realm. The Evangelism department of the Lutheran Church in Madagascar is entitled the "Department of Holy Warfare." This particular charismatic movement originated in the life and ministry of a prophetess, Neni Lava, who through dreams, visions and prayer led a spiritual revival in that Lutheran community. Over ten thousand white-robed "shepherds" have been trained and consecrated for ministries of healing and exorcisms. The authenticity of this Jesus movement is found in forty villages/camps where the diseased and destitute are freely cared for by a compassionate, caring community who integrate spiritual healings with modern medicine. Today 350 million Christians around the world designated Pentecostals trace their roots to Jesus' healing, transforming ministry.

Centers of Empowered Mission

Emil Brunner wrote, "The church is to mission as fire is to burning."[189] That statement is to be made of every expression of the church, including the congregation. The congregation is to mission as fire is to burning. Each congregation is a center of mission. One of the primary purposes of organizing new congregations is to multiply centers of mission.

Christian gatherings are centers of mission. The Holy Spirit through the ministry of Word and Sacrament calls, creates and nurtures ever-new communities of Christians. These persons, empowered by the Holy Spirit, are sent into the world to witness to Jesus crucified in order that centers of Christian proclamation and witness may be multiplied.

The multiplication of centers of Christian witness has been an incredible phenomenon during the last 100 years. In 1900, 87 percent of Christians were found in Europe and the U.S.A. Today over 60 percent of the Jesus movement lives in Latin America, Africa and Asia. "World Christianity" is a fact today and the multiplicity of the Jesus movement is a world reality of which each of us is a part. It transforms senders into receivers and calls the total family to accompany one another in participation in the mission of God, concretized in God's suffering servant and Prince of Peace.

In participating in the mission of the body of Christ, it is always essential that the proclamation of the Cosmic Crucified take place in words and in deeds. We have seen how a theology of the cross fuses forgiveness of sin with actions of and advocacy for righteousness-justice. It is not possible to preach Jesus as Christ and ignore service with the poor, oppressed and marginalized in the world. To do so is a denial of the lordship of Jesus as the Christ.

Witnessing Within Cultural Diversity

As the church accompanies the missioning God across geographical, racial, cultural (including linguistic), and faith boundaries, the gospel of Jesus Christ becomes and must become incarnate within new cultural contexts. In order to communicate with the human community, God becomes human. In order to communicate with specific people, God became incarnate within a specific people. The Son of God was born a specific Jew (of specific Jewish parents), Jesus of Nazareth, who spoke Aramaic, heard and read the ancient Hebrew scriptures and shared their culture and life.

When the early church first moved across cultural and linguistic boundaries, it immediately was aware of the necessity to speak in new languages and to seek for new words and concepts to articulate the meaning of Jesus as the Christ in that new world. In the language of incarnation, the one who is in the form of God emptied himself in order to enter the human sphere. Likewise, the missionary church is called to become aware of its enculturation in order that it might become acculturated in a new time and place. In a sense, the missionary church is called to continually be emptied of its own cultural forms and values in order that it might bear witness to Christ in the new world into which the church is sent.

The very truth of the gospel of Jesus Christ is in part authenticated by its capacity to become actualized in every historical and cultural situation. The New Testament witnesses to this power of the gospel as it broke out of the ancient and traditional Jewish forms and was articulated within a Hellenistic society. The New Testament was written in Greek, not Aramaic, which was the language of Jesus and his disciples. The form and content of the New Testament documents witness to an early church already present and witnessing in a variety of ways within the various contexts of the Roman Empire. Relevance and adaptability to the new missionary situation were a greater priority for the mission of the church than the preservation of a detailed and infallible duplication of the past.

The Nicene Creed, often viewed as a symbol of traditional orthodoxy, actually witnesses to the capacity of the church to empty itself and speak in a new historical and cultural context without denying the reality of God's action in Jesus Christ. The early church exemplifies a missioning church that is a creative, self-emptying people. A static church without capacity to lose its own cultural form is incapable of significant participation in the mission of God.

Effective participation in the mission of the body of Christ is dependent upon the church's willingness to follow the self-emptying Son of God into the world. Once again we are radically challenged to rethink mission within an emphasis on the word and way of Jesus and the Cross.

Contextualization of the Christian Proclamation

At the heart of the Christian faith and mission is the affirmation that God raised Jesus crucified from the dead. The resurrection of Jesus is God's proclamation that Jesus' message is God's message, that Jesus' mission is God's mission. It is the assertion that God has identified Godself in Jesus and there is no God other than the God revealed in Jesus. Jesus is God's greatest gift to humanity for in, with, and through him we have encountered the mystery in which we live and move and have our being (Acts 17).

The confession of the normative nature of Jesus for faith in God is the foundation of our Christian mission; however, this fundamental confession has been articulated in various ways within the history of the Christian community. A brief summary of the development of early church confessions will indicate that the lordship of Jesus was from the beginning confessed authentically in a variety of ways. Each confession was an attempt in a new situation to say that God's authentic and ultimate word had been spoken in Jesus. These confessions make it clear that the church has always been concerned that the confession be both true to Scripture and relevant to the context in which it witnesses.

The New Testament indicates that early statements of faith in Jesus declared that he was a prophet or "the final eschatological prophet." However, within the Jewish community it soon became necessary to describe Jesus as the Messiah in order to claim that it was in Jesus that all the promises of the prophets were fulfilled. However, when early Christianity immediately moved into the Hellenistic environment of the Roman Empire, the title messiah was not effective in expressing the faith of the Christian community. In the Hellenistic world, where the fulfillment of prophecy in the biblical sense was unknown, the confession that Jesus was the Messiah did not signify that the ultimate revelation of Godself and God's purposes was in Jesus. Hellenism determined ultimate truth and life not in terms of the fulfillment of history but in terms of the presence of the divine. The early Christians were compelled to say that Jesus was the divine embodied among us. Jesus was confessed as the Son of God or the incarnation of the Logos of God. "The Word became flesh and lived among us" (John 1.14). In their world of divine emperors and kings it was absolutely necessary that the one in whom God was ultimately revealed be divine. The New Testament witnesses to these early Christian confessions of Jesus' divinity: "Christ Jesus, who, though he was in the form of God, did not regard equality with God as something to be exploited, but emptied himself, taking the form of a slave, being born in human likeness" (Phil 2:5-7).

Even the confessions of Jesus' divinity did not ultimately suffice within the Hellenistic culture, because Hellenism allowed for a variety of "divine" agencies and powers, and Hellenistic philosophy and theology assumed that above creation and the plethora of divine agencies there was the Ultimate One. Because of its perfection that Ultimate One, source of truth and life, did not and could not be related to creation and history. Some early Christians accepted this Hellenistic philosophical principle as ultimate truth. They concluded that the divine incarnate in Jesus was not the Ultimate One but something, although divine, less than the Ultimate God. Therefore, faith in Jesus did not place one in relationship to ultimate truth nor eternal life. The ultimate self-identification of God had not taken place in Jesus.

Others within the early church absolutely refused to accept this conclusion. Their faith forced them to deny and contradict the best philosophical tradition of their day. God, the Ultimate One, was embodied in Jesus. Therefore God could be incarnate in flesh and blood, dust and matter. Faith could affirm that life had been touched with truth and eternity. The Hellenistic environment compelled the fourth-century Christians to say at Nicea that in the incarnation, God of God, light of light, God of very God was and is ultimately present and revealed among us.

As Christians we affirm that we are consciously faithful to this tradition in two respects: 1) The finality of Jesus Christ is to be maintained in our confession and mission. Jesus Christ the crucified and risen servant is the incarnation of God's presence and action in the world. 2) We are also consciously aware, as noted above, that this confession has taken many forms within the history and the traditions of the church. Again and again new situations and contexts call forth new confessions of the Christian faith.

These two presuppositions form the foundation for Christian thinking about the proclamation of the Cosmic Crucified. The one who hung on Calvary has decisive significance for all reality. The discussion has argued that the heart of the universe, God, has defined God's being and mission in this particular Nazarene who in self-giving love was vulnerable unto death. The discussion has also argued that authentic human existence, participating in God's mission in and for the world, is also defined in this same prophetic figure, and therefore all human life and mission is to be conformed to "the one who was rich and became poor." In the Cosmic Crucified is fused the absolute clue to the reality of God and the human community.

How that union of God and human destiny found in the particularity of Jesus crucified is to be articulated, has taken a multiplicity of forms not only within Christian history but in the New Testament itself.[190] The variety of theological formulations is indicative of the fact that what is essential to the Christian faith is not particular Trinitarian statements, but the integral relationship between the story of Jesus and the story of God. The realization of the Reign of God or God's will is defined by a prophetic carpenter who appeared in a back-water Jewish colony of the Roman Empire. God was not to be identified with Imperial Rome, Caesar Augustus, Alexander the Great, Hellenistic philosophers as Plato and Aristotle, but with a humble carpenter whose searing insight exposed the hypocrisy of the political and religious elite and whose courage and heart seemingly replicated the heavenly Father to whom he surrendered. The ministry of Jesus began with crowds of weak, poor, diseased and alienated who welcomed a voice of compassion and truth as originating in the God of Israel. However, that ministry soon changed to a tragic mission in which Jesus' embodiment of truth became a tragic mission of crucified truth. All of our relative confessions witness repeatedly to Jesus as crucified truth. The most awesome and wondrous is eventually embodied in crucified Truth. That is the heart of Christianity. In the words of Herbert Butterfied quoted earlier, "Hold to Christ and for everything else be totally uncommitted!"[191]

A Theological Proposal

In an earlier study distributed by the Division for World Mission and Inter-Church Cooperation of the former American Lutheran Church (DWMIC/ALC),[192] it was suggested that within a Muslim world it might be helpful to study and explore the effectiveness of witnessing to God's final word to humanity in terms of Jesus as the crucified and raised prophet. Robert W. Jenson wrote an insightful and creative essay entitled "The Risen Prophet." In it he suggested "that faith's necessary affirmations about Christ can in the Islamic context be made by calling him the 'Risen Prophet.'"[193] Jenson argues that the Nicene confession responded to the question "May not God be different for and in himself" than God appears in Jesus Christ?[194] Arians argued that God was different from Jesus Christ. The Son was only like the Father. God had not ultimately identified Godself in the Son.

The Nicene Creed, in response to various forms of Arianism, stated precisely the opposite, "*that Christ is homousios 'of one being' with 'the Father'*" and therefore God has identified God's own being and future in Jesus Christ. Jenson calls this Nicea's "trinitarian move."[195]

Jenson then continues by suggesting that the same "trinitarian move" might be made within Islam by speaking of Jesus as the "Risen Prophet." The question remains the same, "Might not God be different for and in himself" than what God speaks through the prophet? The fact that God raised Jesus from the dead is God's self-authentication of the prophetic voice of Jesus. God has identified himself in this particular risen prophet. In Nicene terms, this means that the prophetic word is uncreated, belonging to the essential being of God. Jenson notes that Muslims have been open to discussing the nature of the Qur'an in this way.

Finally, Jenson suggests that if Muslims might begin to think of Jesus as the "Risen Prophet" that would not be the end of the discussion. Future Christians within Muslim communities might be driven to ask questions similar to those that engendered the Nicene formulation. How that discussion might be carried on and to what it might lead can only be determined by future Muslims who might possibly be grasped in faith by the Cosmic Crucified.

God and Jesus: Theological Reflections for Christian-Muslim Dialog was developed by DWMIC/ALC as a document to explore possibilities for the contextualization of theology within the Muslim community. There was no indication that this was the only or best articulation of the faith within the Muslim world. It simply argued that it might be effective to speak of the Cosmic Crucified within the Muslim world in terms of the prophetic role common to both Muslims and Christians.

There was also no suggestion that the new terminology removed fundamental differences in how Christians and Muslims understand the reality of God. The document stated, "The validity of this document does not depend upon its value in convincing Muslims to be Christians, but in possibly clarifying for Muslims and Christians how we believe in one God differently."[196] This discussion has been noted in order to indicate that even as flexibility and creativity are apparent in the early church's witness documented in the New Testament, so they are also needed today as Christians explore how they might witness to Jesus, the Cosmic Crucified among people of other faiths.[197]

Religious Pluralism: Exploring Options for New Relationships

Religious pluralism and interfaith relationships have become a fact of life for our own culture and society. Previous generations experienced religious pluralism as a distant reality separated by oceans and alien cultures. Today religious pluralism is integral to our own communities. Immigration patterns, international political realities, and developments in communication technology place religious pluralism at our doorstep. Interfaith relationships are no longer relegated to international specialists but are the possibility and responsibility of us all.

September 11, 2001 has created a tremendous interest in religious pluralism, particularly Islam. For many, Islam represents a false or demonic religion among us. For others, Islam represents a religious community grounded in deep moral values which at one point in history represented the best in world civilization. How do we begin to understand the variety of Christian responses to religious diversity? The purpose of this article is to describe and respond to a number of theological models which express various understandings of how Christians relate to "the religious other." This theological journey may enable us to explore our own attitudes and thoughts and thereby inform our own interfaith journey.

Religious Pluralism

A Sociological Fact

Religious pluralism is a sociological fact. There are approximately 2.2 billion Christians around the globe, 1.2. billion Muslims, 800 million Hindus, 350 million Buddhists, 1 billion secularists, 100 million Traditionalists, and many others including 13 million Jews.

Within the city of Chicago there are 350,000 Muslims, 170,000 Hindus, 130,000 Buddhists, and 200,000 Jews. Religious pluralism is increasingly a reality in our own communities. Our doctor is often an Indian Hindu, our children play soccer with Muslim children, the local banker may be a Buddhist.

A Positive or Negative Reality?

Religious pluralism is not simply a sociological fact; rather, it is experienced by the pluralistic community from a variety of perspectives. For some people, religious pluralism makes a positive contribution to their community. New values, new insights, new experiences, and new relationships add color to the multicolored tapestry which is the religiously plural community. For other people religious pluralism is a threat to the community. Diverse religious commitments are immediately seen as undermining the stability of society or as a threat to national security. This has been particularly evident in the U.S.A. after 9/11. Many U.S. citizens understand the U.S. to be a "Christian" country and find the presence of Muslims, Hindus and Buddhists a threat to national unity and security. Others understand "alien" religions to be demonic. A number of statements from evangelical Fundamentalists such as Franklin Graham and Jerry Falwell reflect this fear of pluralism. For others there may be both a joy in finding a more inclusive human community and a wariness concerning the stability and security of the community and nation. This is simply to say religious pluralism is not simply a fact.

A Philosophical/Theological Relativism

Discussions concerning inter-faith relationships and dialogue seem inevitably to end in discussions about the "finality" or "normativity" of one faith's vision and the faith visions of other communities. For some, even to make a positive comment about another religious tradition or people is to some extent a denial of one's own faith and tradition. The revelatory events of one's own faith are unique, absolute and final. This implies that one religion is superior and worthy of trust. Any positive statement about other religions may appear to threaten or undermine the faith foundation upon which we trust our lives. Philosophical and theological relativism must be denied if faith is to be certain and secure.

Relativism in contrast to ultimate truth is a primary presupposition of what is designated Post-Modernism. Traditional orthodoxy found truth in the past in revelation, sacred scriptures and doctrine. Modernism rejected revelatory and ecclesiastical authority, claiming that the only authority was reason. Modernism assumed that reality was one and rational and therefore truth was discoverable by the human mind.

Post-Modernism rejects both orthodoxy and Modernism and their claims to final truth. For the Post-Modernist, all reality and knowledge of reality is a social construct. Human communities and cultures, through thought, intuition and imagination, create the worlds, the "sacred canopies," in which we live.[198] Each community, each culture is unique, being the consequence of a particular historical context and movement. Each culture, community, from their own time and place has a particular perspective from which they view their reality. Each community has their own particular criteria for truth, a truth that serves them well or is denied. In a Post-Modern world there is a multiplicity of truths relative to each context. Claims to find one final religious truth are considered inappropriate or even absurd.

Three Models for Understanding Interfaith Relationships

Generalization and in this case interpretive models are always questionable because they oversimplify and fail to capture the nuances made by particular perspectives. On the other hand models are helpful in interpreting a vast amount of material and making comparisons possible. In contemporary theological discussion three models are often used in interpreting the discussion concerning the relationships between Christianity and people of other faiths. They are exclusivism, inclusivism and pluralism.

The Exclusivist Model

The Christian exclusivist is convinced that there is one final revelation of God and one ultimate saving event of God, namely Jesus Christ. There is one true saving religion. There is no revelation or saving activity of God in other religions. Salvation is not a possibility outside the preaching of Christ and faith in Jesus Christ. However, there may be glimpses of truth in other religions.

In the year 2000 at the invitation of Dr. Billy Graham 10,000 evangelical theologians, evangelists, mission strategists and church leaders from 200 countries gathered to study, discuss and pray about the continuing task of world evangelization. Out of that meeting came The Amsterdam Declaration. In this document, there is a brief statement on Religious Pluralism and Evangelism which illustrates Christian exclusivism. It reads,

> Today's evangelist is called to proclaim the gospel in an increasingly pluralist world. In this global village of competing faiths and many world religions, it is important that our evangelism is marked both by faithfulness to the good news of Christ and humility in our delivery of it. Because God's general revelation extends to all points of his creation, there may well be traces of truth, beauty and goodness in many non-Christian belief systems. But we have no warrant for regarding any of them as alternative gospels or separate roads to salvation. The only way to know God in peace, love and joy is through the reconciling death of Jesus Christ the risen Lord.[199]

An earlier section of the Declaration places this statement within the context of Christ's judgment. "Therefore all human beings now face final condemnation by Christ the judge, and eternal destruction, separated from the presence of the Lord."[200]

There are a variety of theological positions within what is designated as exclusivism. There are Fundamentalists who would deny traces of truth outside of Christ or claim that other religious expressions are demonic (Jerry Falwell). On the other hand there are persons sometimes categorized as exclusivists who believe that God's saving event, Christ, has saving implications beyond the preaching of the Gospel (Karl Barth). The Amsterdam Declaration expresses an exclusivist position that not only avoids the extremes within the model but represents the faith of millions of "Evangelical" Christians that are major voices within the United States.

The Inclusivist Model

The Inclusivist believes that Christ is God's normative revelation or God's universally saving event; however, in contrast to the exclusivist, God's revealing and saving power is present within all history and within every culture and people.

The Inclusivist Representative Model

The Roman Catholic theologian, Karl Rahner, is placed within this model. Rahner trusts that God is love and desires that all humanity know salvation. In order to achieve this Rahner believes that all human life is divinely gifted with what he calls "the supernatural existential." This gift enables all humanity to be open or closed to the grace of God and manifest or distort the gifts of God. Jesus is the final/ultimate revelation because Jesus is the human who is fully open to the presence and saving power of God. In this Christ, one sees that reality which is potentially a reality in every human being. Rahner sees the "supernatural existential" as a universal gift and therefore God's grace may break through everywhere, even among other religions.

> Every human being is really and truly exposed to the influence of divine, supernatural grace, which offers an interior union with God and by means of which God communicates himself whether the individual takes up an attitude of acceptance or refusal towards this grace.[201]

Rahner is convinced that supernatural grace at work within those open to grace is found throughout human history and religions. This means that

> Christianity does not simply confront the members of extra-Christian religions as a mere non-Christian but as someone who can and might already be regarded in this or that respect as an anonymous Christian.[202]

Jesus Christ is the normative expression of the saving God who is universally present, saving and acting including within other religions. Grace comes to full expression in Jesus Christ.

Rahner's inclusivist model is sometimes called the "representative/expressive" inclusivist model. The Roman Catholic theologian Hans Küng develops his thinking from Rahner's theological position. Following another Catholic theologian, Heinz Robert Schlette, Küng speaks of the world religions as God's ordinary means of salvation. The traditions, symbols, events, and words within religious communities have grown out of a people's openness to God's grace. Therefore God uses those gifts as means of transforming or saving people through God's grace. Christianity, however, is the extraordinary means of salvation because Christ is the fullest and normative expression of the grace. That normative faith will be shared by the church with all humanity.[203]

Pope John Paul II was not enthusiastic about this development within Catholic theology and rejected the terminology "ordinary" and extra-ordinary religion.[204] In the recent "Dominus Iesus," the Vatican found it fitting to add this conditional statement: "If it is true that the followers of other religions can receive divine grace, it is also certain that 'objectively speaking' they are in a gravely deficient situation in comparison to those who, in the church, have the fullness of the means of salvation."[205]

The Inclusive Instrumental/Constitutive Model

The inclusive instrumental model articulates the view that Christ is God's final revelation and God's ultimate saving event. God not only comes to expression in Christ but God does something new in this saving event, the effects of which may be understood as encompassing the whole of humanity and creation. What distinguishes this view from the exclusivist model is that there is a much greater appreciation for God's revelatory and saving activity outside the traditional house of faith. The Word, or Logos of God, which became incarnate in Jesus Christ, is recognized as the Word of God which permeates all creation. Wherever wisdom, truth, love, justice and beauty appear it is recognized as the "general" revelation of God. This "general" revelation appears under the cultural forms and patterns of all religions. The Biblical traditions are replete with the identification of God outside the household of faith. Melchizidek, a Caananite priest of the Most High God, blessed Abraham;[206] Proverbs 8 recognized the presence of Wisdom, the co-creator of reality, as the source of justice among all the kings and nobles of the earth.[207] Paul recognizes the conscience seared into the fabric of humanity as the voice of God and concludes "and their conflicting thoughts will accuse or perhaps excuse them on the day, when, according to my Gospel, God, through Jesus Christ will judge the secret thoughts of all."[208] In Matthew 25:31ff, in the parable of the last judgment, Jesus states that humanity from all corners of the earth will be judged by how they responded to their neighbor in need, not knowing that the Son of Man is present though hidden there.

Some theologians would make further affirmations of God's revealing and saving work outside the household of faith. They would proclaim the Christ in order that people might be saved but would also recognize that the saving work of God in Christ may very well incorporate people from outside the household of faith into God's kingdom. However, although they would hope for that inclusion through the saving act of God in Jesus Christ, they would leave the reality of that inclusion in the hands of the Mystery of God.[209]

Wolfhart Pannenberg and Carl Braaten develop a definite inclusive constitutive/instrumental model. They both see God as active within all of history and within every culture. All the religions of the world are traditions in which God is active. This Biblical God is the God of the future in which all of cosmic life will be transformed and where righteousness, love, truth and justice will be realized. Since God is universally active, people within all religious traditions are in a sense the "footprints" of God within history.

However, Braaten and Pannenberg see Jesus Christ not only as the revealing event but the saving event within this historical process. Within the Jewish tradition with its eschatological hopes Christ proclaims the coming reign of God, the hope that all of life is and will be transformed. Within this mission Jesus is crucified but most significantly God raises Jesus from the dead. The resurrection is God's vindication of Jesus' mission and message. The future which Jesus proclaimed is guaranteed by God's raising Jesus. In Paul's terms Jesus is the first "fruit" of those to be raised from the dead. In Braaten and Pannenberg's terms, God's future resurrection is now a present reality and identifies the future of all of history.

All religions moving towards God's future will eventually be incorporated into the eschatological future of God. Furthermore, Christians recognize the presence of God when they see the hungry fed, the naked clothed, the prisoners visited and thirsty given something to drink[210] and recognize that the present and hidden Son of Man is being responded to. Furthermore, this model makes clear that the saving activity of God in Christ will be universally effective in incorporating all of history within God's grace.[211]

The National Council of the Churches of Christ in the U.S.A. incorporates both the exclusivist model and the inclusivist model into its statement, "Interfaith Relations and the Churches." One section of the document reads:

> Jesus Christ is also the focus of the most vexing questions regarding how Christians understand their relationship with men and women of other religions. Christians agree that God incarnated and incarnates still—the inexhaustible love and salvation that reconciles us all. We agree that it is not by any merit of our own, but by God's grace and our faithful response that we are reconciled. Likewise, Christians also agree that our discipleship impels us to become reconciled to the whole human family and to live in proper relationship to all God's creation. We disagree, however, on whether non-Christians may be reconciled to God, and if so, how. Many Christians see no

possibility of reconciliation with God apart from a conscious acceptance of Jesus Christ as incarnate Son of God and personal savior [the exclusivist model]. For others, the reconciling work of Jesus is salvific in its own right, independent of any particular human response [an instrumental inclusivist model].[212]

The Pluralist Model: Ramblings Along the Rubicon

The exclusivist and inclusivist models have been challenged by the pluralist model which insists that Christianity is not meant to be Christo-centric but Theo-centric; theology is not centered in Christ but in the Reality of God, particularly in a common experience of the Mystery of God. Jesus Christ is one of many revealing and saving events that originate and spring forth from the one Reality of God. Other religions are ways of salvation without reference to Christ. There is no normative Christology.

Professor John Hick, formerly professor of Philosophy of Religion at Claremont Graduate School in California, is widely recognized as a leading spokesperson of this model. Professor Paul Knitter, a Catholic lay theologian, has been another highly recognized advocate of this model. Knitter in 1985 published a now famous volume, *No Other Name? A Critical Survey of Christian Attitudes Toward the World Religions*[213] in which he writes an excellent survey of the various Interfaith Christian models. Within that survey he argues for a theology committed to a non-normative Christology within what he designates as "unitive pluralism." Knitter assumed that the reality of the one Mystery comes to expression in a variety of religious revelations and manifestations. Dialogue is needed to explore the Truth behind all religious truths, that is, a "unitive pluralism." Both Knitter and John Hick were convinced that the exclusivist and inclusivist models with their assertion of the finality of Jesus Christ resulted in Christian arrogance and imperialism which was divisive of humanity and made authentic dialogue between Christians and people of other faiths impossible. Furthermore, there were challenges from philosophy, psychology and the study of world religions which demanded a re-thinking of the relationship between peoples of faith.

In 1987 Orbis Books published a volume in their Faith Meets Faith series entitled *The Myth of Christian Uniqueness: Toward a Pluralistic Theology of Religions.*[214] The editors of the book were John Hick and Paul Knitter, and the essays emerged from a conference held at the

Claremont Graduate School, Claremont, California, March 7-8, 1986. In the Preface to the book, Paul Knitter writes that the conference attempted to bring together people with "new understandings" of the relationship between Christianity and other religions. Knitter wrote:

'New understandings' were described as any effort to move beyond the two general models that have dominated Christian attitudes towards other religions up to the present: the 'conservative' exclusivist approach, which finds salvation only in Christ and little, if any, value elsewhere; and the 'liberal' inclusivist attitude, which recognizes the salvific richness of other faiths but then views this richness as the result of Christ's redemptive work and as having to be fulfilled in Christ. We wanted to gather theologians who were exploring the possibilities of a pluralistic position – a move away from the insistence on the superiority or finality of Christ and the recognition of the independent validity of other ways. Such a move came to be described by participants in our project as the crossing of a theological Rubicon.[215]

Participants described this shift in theological perspective as: "a 'monstrous shift' (Langdon Gilkey), a 'fundamental revision' (Gordon Kaufmann), 'genetic-like mutation' (Raimunds Panniker), 'a momentous Kairos' (Knitter), a 'Copernican Revolution' and 'radical transformation' (Hick)."[216]

It is interesting to note that the original crossing of the Rubicon from Gaul to Italy (north to south) in 49 B.C.E. by the General Julius Caesar was understood by the Roman Senate as an act of war. The Claremont gathering no doubt recognized that their assertion of a new pluralistic approach to interfaith relationships would be recognized by many within the Christian churches as an attack on the traditional faith. The Claremont gathering probably had visions similar to Julius Caesar of taking over the empire.

The essays in *The Myth of Christian Uniqueness* are divided into three bridges used to cross the theological Rubicon in challenging the traditional faith of Christian churches.

a. The Historic-Cultural Bridge: Relativity

Cultural and historical relativism assumes that every cultural and historical expression or event is limited by and relative to a particular time and place. No event, truth or revelation transcends this relativism and cannot be used to norm another event, truth or revelation. "All of these diverse conceptions and pictures (from cultural and religious traditions)seem best understood as the product of human imaginative creativity in the face of the mystery that life is to all of us."[217]

b. The Theologic-Mystical Bridge: Mystery

It would appear that one underlying, hidden, inner divine Mystery comes to expression in every religion. Every religion partially expresses this Mystery. "The object or content of authentic religious experience is infinite—Mystery beyond all forms, exceeding our every grasp of it.[218]

c. The Ethico-Practical Bridge: Justice

The third bridge to pluralism is not "a consciousness of historical relativity or absolute Mystery, but the confrontation with the suffering of humanity and the need to end such outrages."[219] The argument is that religious claims to superiority lead to attitudes of superiority resulting in conflict, domination, and exploitation. Rosemary Radford Ruether writes: "[Christianity's] commandments of love and universal fellowship between people evidently have not served as a check on this internecine warfare. Crusades, witch-hunts, religious wars, and pogroms have all been a part of this violent, chauvinistic history of Christianity."[220] Justice and compassion are to be found in the renunciation of "finality" and the willingness of all religious communities to cooperate in overcoming the problems which produce poverty, violence and oppression.

These are the three bridges that lead to "pluralism." From the perspective of more traditional understandings of interfaith relationships, the bridges are seen as basic challenges to "finality claims." Returning to the image of crossing the Rubicon, what Julius Caesar saw as tools (bridges) to challenge the power of the Roman Senate, the Senate saw as an act of war.

d. An Inclusive Response to the Pluralist Model

In 1992, Orbis published another book in the Faith Meets Faith series, entitled *Christian Uniqueness Reconsidered: The Myth of a Pluralistic Theology of Religions*, edited by Gavin D'Costa. The essays in this volume in a variety of ways question and challenge the pluralistic model advocated in *The Myth of Christian Uniqueness*. Gavin D'Costa writes in the preface:

> One of the purposes of this book is to help indicate that the Rubicon is a deeper and more treacherous river than

initially recognized. We have also wanted to show that there are many other creative, imaginative and socially sensitive ways in which Christian theology can proceed in its encounter with the world religions.[221]

Within the fourteen essays representative of the inclusive model, a number of challenges are made to the pluralists. First, several authors question whether there actually is a common religious or psychological experience or one "Holy Other" lying behind the multiplicity of religious experiences within humanity. Furthermore, is it possible to separate the so-called inner kernel of religious experience from the cultural outer husks of that experience? Particularly in a post-modern world this question has a contemporary legitimacy. The question is crucial for Paul Knitter and John Hick because their theological argument is based on the assumption that one ultimate Reality is the whence of all authentic religious experience.[222]

A second challenge to the pluralist model is that in its quest to make dialogue possible between peoples of faith it actually prevents dialogue from happening. For example, Christianity, Islam and Buddhism all make claims to finality of Truth. True dialogue is possible when people are accepted and dialogue within their claims to finality. Several contributors argue that what pluralists actually do is to create a new faith of "unitive pluralists." This new faith believes that One Reality and one religious experience is common to all humanity. Critics of pluralism do not see "unitive pluralism" as a unifying, underlying religious experience which must be accepted before peoples of faith can dialogue with each other. The critics argue that it is more honest and helpful to accept our differences including our different truth claims and enter into dialogue with them. [223]

Third, a few authors point out that normative claims to finality do not necessarily lead to imperialistic, exploitive or oppressive attitudes and actions.[224] In my book *The Word and Way of the Cross* I argue that it should be quite the opposite. If Christians truly are conformed to the cruciformed mission of Christ, the way of the cross cannot be imperialistic, but is the way of creative, suffering servanthood. To be great in the Kingdom of God is to walk with and as the least within the story of the Reign of God (Mk 10:35-45).[225]

Fourth, a few critics state that the relativism within the Pluralistic Model may lead to ethical and moral chaos. Interestingly enough, Langdon Gilkey, in the original volume *The Myth of Christian Uniqueness*, made this point. Gilkey noted that within the necessity of recognizing the place of relativity within culture and religion, we are confronted by horrendous evil as, for example, in Nazi Germany. One recognizes immediately that in this confrontation one needs a rock (an absolute) upon which to stand in order to name and challenge the demonic powers which destroy life.[226] At the same time there is a need for caution (a recognition of our relative perspective) lest we participate in an oppressive religious absolutism.

Fifth, many authors argue that Christianity cannot be understood apart from the claims to finality which are made for Jesus Christ in the New Testament. This is stated in response to the Pluralists who assert that the New Testament claims for Jesus' finality are relative to the context of first century Christianity. The authors of this volume believe that Christianity should continue to make normative claims about Jesus Christ.

Within the critique of pluralism the authors share insights and make suggestions as to how the Christian community might go about relating to persons of other faiths. This essay will not explore those suggestions but follow the impact which this critique made on Paul Knitter and the Pluralist Model, and which led to two other interfaith-models.

The Emergence of Knitter's Correlational Model

Paul Knitter became the author of what he called the "correlational model." The Orbis Faith Meets Faith series not only made possible this dialogue concerning interfaith relationships but also facilitated the emergence of the correlational model through its publication of three volumes which focused upon the work of Knitter: *The Uniqueness of Jesus: A Dialogue with Paul Knitter; One Earth Many Religions: Multifaith Dialogue and Global Responsibility; and Jesus and the Other Names: Christian Mission and Global Responsibility.*[227]

In concluding *One Earth Many Religions*, Knitter writes,

I've tried to make a case that the best way to carry on a multifaith dialogue that will encourage all the participants to relate to each other in a conversation in which everyone genuinely speaks and listens to each other is to base such a dialogue on a shared commitment to promoting eco-human well being of Earth and Humanity.[228]

The statement indicates the direction in which Knitter's thought has turned.

First, Knitter increasingly focused his understanding o and Christianity on the pain and suffering of people and creaᴜᴏᴜ. He speaks of moving from Christocentrism to Theocentrism and finally to soteriocentrism which focuses upon the transformation of a suffering people and world, a movement to global responsibility.[230] As part of that move Knitter accepts the critics' challenge that dialogue cannot be rooted in the acceptance of a common experience of Mystery lying behind all religious phenomena. "Rather than presuppose a common core for all individually wrapped religious experience (since we cannot discard the wrapping), I am now following the lead of those who hold up 'salvation' or 'wellbeing' of humans and earth, as the starting point."[231]

Second, Knitter speaks of a correlational model emphasizing the need of conversation, of listening, of relationships, of receiving as well as giving, in which all participants are given equal rights and treated equally.[232]

At this point Knitter has again listened to his critics and has moved from insisting that dialogue must begin with an assumption of religious parity to an equal voice and place in the conversation.[233] Within the parameters of Knitter's concern for dialogue and global responsibility he develops the theological framework of his correlational model.

Knitter again has listened to his critics who have challenged his earlier non-normative Christology as not only non-Biblical but irrelevant to a world in which moral evil is confronted. Knitter develops then a multi-normative approach to religious pluralism. In developing this approach Knitter argues that the uniqueness of Jesus as the revelation of God is not that Jesus is the full, definitive and unsurpassable revelation of God, but Jesus is the universal, decisive and indispensable revelation of God. Jesus is not the full revelation because this is not only idolatrous (identifying the finite and infinite) but limits God from revelation at other time and places. However, Jesus' revelation is universal in having meaning for people in all times and places. Furthermore, the revelation of God in Jesus is not definitive or unsurpassable since either category restricts/limits God. However, Jesus is decisive in that he shakes and challenges us and Jesus is indispensable in that we need this revelation to be truly fulfilled. Knitter summarizes this perspective by saying Jesus is truly but not solely the revelation of God.[234] Knitter continues by noting that there is the probability that there are other universal, decisive and indispensable revelations of God[235] and Christians are to be open to being enriched within the process of inter-faith relationships. However, Knitter is confident that these revelations will not contradict each other.[236]

Knitter was also impacted by fellow Catholic theologians who questioned the orthodoxy of his pluralistic approach. Responding to his critics, Knitter writes, "Christians must continue to proclaim Jesus as savior and divine.... But what do these announcements mean? And how can Christians continue to make these proclama-tions in such a way that they maintain the uniqueness of Jesus without closing themselves to the uniqueness of other religious figures and revelations?"[237] Knitter believes that he can do this on the basis of a representational Christology rather than a constitutive Christology. In the latter God does something new through Jesus Christ through which salvation is realized, whereas in the representational Christology Jesus reveals something that is already universally present and active. Within the representational view Knitter can say that Jesus is savior and divine.[238] In this sense Jesus is a primordial sacra-ment. Within this context Knitter can also say, "Then I can recognize that the love of God (revealed in Jesus) is broader than Jesus and can, perhaps, be revealed elsewhere in different but equally effec-tive ways."[239]

With this discussion Knitter emphasizes that within our contem-porary context Jesus is to be primarily understood as an agent of the liberating Kingdom of God. In *The Uniqueness of Jesus* Knitter writes,

> The content of Jesus' uniqueness must be made clear in Christian life and witness. This content, however, will be understood and proclaimed differently in different con-texts and periods of history. Today, the uniqueness of Jesus can be found in his insistence that salvation or the Reign of God must be realized in this world through human actions of love and justice.[240]

This is the basic thesis in Knitter's new approach to dialogue. He writes, "Unless we are realizing salvation or well-being in and for this world we are not announcing the salvation announced by Jesus. This is the unique ingredient in his saving message."[241] Knitter was deeply moved by a visit to India in 1991 where he witnessed the incredible poverty and suffering which exists there. He has also been influenced by the Asian, Latin American and feminist theolo-gians who, writing within the context of oppression and suffering, have been grasped by the Biblical emphasis upon liberation, justice and transformation of life.

Finally, it needs to be noted that Knitter understands his theological language concerning Christ to be performative or action language. That is, to confess Jesus as Lord is to walk in discipleship in faithful obedience to Jesus' revelation of the Kingdom of God.

A Response to Knitter's Correlational Model

Knitter can be deeply appreciated for his capacity to listen and respond to theological positions that challenge his own theology. His correlational model, from my perspective, is a much more adequate model than his original pluralistic model in *No Other Name?*. However, I would still have several questions and additions (as follows).

Several writers have indicated that Knitter's criteria for the uniqueness of Jesus are very limited. The criterion, to a large extent, is confined to Jesus' announcement of the Kingdom of God active within history for the purpose of the transformation of history and life. This transformation results in justice and meaningful life for all. While fully appreciating the major significance of this approach and without minimizing the truth of this insight, it is also a fact that there are other dimensions of Jesus that contribute profoundly to his uniqueness and molding of the Christian faith. Another dimension would be Jesus' Spirituality as a Spirit-called, empowered, led, possessed and eventually raised person. Knitter's remarks concerning Jesus as a sacrament would indicate that he would be in agreement with this observation. Furthermore, from my Lutheran perspective it must be clearly stated that Jesus' relationships with all people, whether marginalized, poor, condemned, oppressed, oppressor, or sinner was a relationship which flowed from an absolutely unconditional love. This unconditional love made table-fellowship with "sinners" not only possible, but from Jesus' perspective a God necessitated participation in the Kingdom's mission. This unconditional love also made unreliable, failing, deserting and betraying disciples candidates for missionary status within the body of Christ as instruments within the Kingdom of God.

From my own perspective Knitter also has a problem when he insists that the saving/revealing event of Jesus Christ is surpassable. Knitter does qualify this statement by saying that Christians are confident that other revelations will not contradict that which is incarnate in Jesus Christ. However, he so limits the criteria for Jesus' uniqueness and is so open to differences (for example he does not seem to see any contradiction or incompatibility between the life visions of Christianity and Buddhism, a question which will be considered by Mark Heim) that I, and many others, question whether this perspective might be vulnerable to losing powerful dimensions of the faith. I, for example, would absolutely insist that "unsurpassable" means that God will never be any other than the God concretized in Jesus Christ. God will never be other than Jesus' Abba who in costly and pain-filled love passionately is wrapped up in a broken and suffering world. The God who is even willing in God's self and through Jesus Christ to go through death and hell in order that forgiveness and new life might spring forth from death, and joy and hope might bubble forth from the desert of human existence. It is this love that embraces all reality, permeates all existence, which makes all life possible and is the source of God's revealing and saving presence and activity.

Finally, Knitter as well as many other contemporary Christian theologians have problems in working out their new theologies because of the manner in which they have reinterpreted the resurrection. Knitter makes it very clear in his book, *No Other Name* (see pp. 199-200), that he interprets the resurrection in terms of subjective/objective visions which have a transforming effect upon the early disciples. He states that this is similar to the way in which the Buddha has transformed the life of his followers. This interpretation does not adequately account for the experience of the early witnesses as reported in the New Testament; nor does it account for the emerging theology of the cross which places the darkness of Good Friday within the heart of God; nor does it account for the boldness and courage of the early disciples as they were tormented and crucified by the Roman Empire.

The Pluralism of Salvation Model

S. Mark Heim in a 1995 volume, *Salvation: Truth and Difference in Religion* (also an Orbis "Faith Meets Faith" publication), develops a thorough critique of the "pluralistic model." Heim's basic challenge is that pluralism, contrary to its own intent, does not take pluralism seriously. Pluralism does not truly accept the religious diversity within world religions, but seeks for a universal unifying religious reality beneath the surface of religious phenomena. Heim analyzes the work of three pluralists as he develops his own position. John Hick presupposes one "Reality," one "Wholly Other" which comes to expression in a variety of faith expressions; Cantwell Smith finds one "faith attitude/orientation" behind a variety of faith expressions; Paul Knitter insists that all religions seek for a common "eco-human justice" which makes religious dialogue possible and effective.

Heim notes that these pluralists insist that interfaith dialogue and relationships are possible on the basis that one ignores the religious particulars and finds a unifying reality beneath the surface. Heim argues that this search for an abstract reality lying behind or below the particulars is a Western cultural product and that for the pluralist this abstract reality, not the actual religious expressions, represents religious truth. This Western philosophical approach does not have to take particular religious traditions seriously.[242]

Dialogue is not a dialogue between particular religious perspectives but between those who recognize the "true reality" that unites humanity and the cosmos. In his analysis Heim notes the questionability of seeking to distinguish between religious phenomena and abstract reality[243] and also notes that what pluralists actually achieve is to create one more religious community among the world religions.[244] We noted similar critiques in an earlier discussion; however, Heim is to be commended for the thoroughness of his argument.

In contrast to the pluralistic model, Heim seeks "to find a fruitful way of combining recognition of truth or validity *and* difference across religions.... A perspective is needed which can recognize the effective truth of what is truly other."[245]

Heim develops his appreciation for "the other" through a philosophical perspective advanced by Nicholas Rescher called "orientational pluralism." In contrast to claims that there is one truth, no truth or partial and complementary truths, Rescher claims that within our given reality all observations and assertions concerning that reality are made from a particular perspective. Observers viewing from different perspectives see different things. Their assertions may seem to conflict and contradict; however, their assertions may all be true from their various perspectives.[246]

Heim uses this insight to advocate for the validity of a legitimate religious diversity and the possibility of a variety of religious perspectives. In seeking a hypothesis which may affirm most adequately the differences within religious traditions, Heim proposes that religious aims, fulfillments, or forms of salvation are various. "In my view the key to such an effort [understanding religious pluralism] is an emphasis on the fulfillment of various religious ends."[247]

Heim argues that there is an organic, integral relationship be-tween a religious perspective and practice with the end sought as fulfillment of life. **"There should be some integral relationship be-tween future human states and present ones, else the universe is organized neither with the principles of equity we recognize nor with the processes of development we can conceive. I agree with this con-tention."**[248] Heim goes on to state that different religious traditions affirm different religious goals. Christians seek communion with the Triune God; Buddhists seek Nirvana. Within Heim's views of the multiplicity of perspectives the goals of communion with the Triune God and Nirvana are not contradictory. "True, they cannot both be true at the same time for the same person. But for different people, or the same person at different times, there is no necessary contra-diction in both being true."[249] Heim argues that a diversity of religious goals (salvation) is the case for humanity within the historical plane but also for post-death experience if this be the reality.[250] Since a variety of human fulfillments are possible, Heim writes:

> I suggest that Christians can consistently recognize that some traditions encompass religious ends which are states of human transformation, distinct from that Christians seek.... The crucial question among the faiths is not 'which one saves?' but 'what counts as salvation?'[251]

From Heim's own Christian Trinitarian perspective he sees the multiplicity of religious ends as made possible within the plentitude of God. Heim lives within the Trinitarian tradition in which God's self-revelation in Christ widens the scope of God's grace and in which the co-eternality of the Spirit, which blows where the Spirit wills, makes relationships with peoples of other faiths vital. Furthermore the Trinitarian focus upon communion and loving relationships and Jesus' own self-giving love requires interfaith dialogue and commu-nity seeking for justice.[252] Heim finds Knitter's emphasis upon justice to be valuable, linking religious reality to historical existence in ways that other pluralists fail to do.[253]

Heim's critique of religious pluralism is incisive; however, his assertion of a plurality of religious goals not only within history but beyond death is questionable. One cannot question that the aims/goals of a religion mold present experience, practice and thought. The goal of the Theravada Buddhist leads to endless hours of medi-tation seeking the liberated self. However, to move from the present to the other side of death is highly questionable. Heim's argument is based upon salvation as primarily an individual event and the result of an individual's achievement. It appears that the major premise for this assertion is that if this were not true then "the universe is organized neither in accord with principles of equity we recognize nor with the processes of development we conceive."[254] Heim continually speaks of religious fulfillment as something to be achieved and within this definition of "salvation" he argues for the necessity of equity and developmental process.

From my own Christian perspective God's action within and fulfillment of life is not an achievement but an absolutely gracious, surprising gift. It is a costly gift offered from God's love and God's freedom. This costly gift, which is loose in the cosmos, is concretized in Jesus Christ crucified and raised. As a radically surprising gift it need not recognize equity or developmental process. This is precisely the point of Jesus parable of the laborers in the vineyard (Mt 20, 1-16); and Paul's understanding of justification by grace through faith. This is total divine love which is poured out upon all creation and all humanity and in spite of our religious goals and achievements will fulfill a transformed humanity with awesome joy transcending all heavens, paradises, and Nirvanas.[255] Heim's model, although developed within a Christian theological world, has more in common with the Hindu understanding of "karma" where for every action there is necessarily a reaction. From Heim's perspective, one creates one's own future rather than receiving one's future as a gift.

Furthermore, Heim's conclusions would seem to lead to the absurd conclusion that any life on the other side of death is compartmentalized into a heavenly mansion for Buddhists, another for Muslims, another for Hindus and another for Christians , etc. This polysalvationism would affirm that human visions rather than God's transforming grace will create the future of the universe. I would interpret the Jesus of the Gospel of John to say that in my Father's house there are many rooms/mansions, therefore there will be room for all of you. Jesus is not saying "fear not, here you will not be disturbed by members of different religious communities !"

Concluding Remarks

This journey along the contemporary theological Rubicon has made possible a survey of a number of theological models for understanding interfaith relationships. My own reflections have appeared in portions of the journey and indicate that I may be located somewhere within the inclusivist camp. Three major factors place me there.

One, I am convinced that the Abba and Spirit of Jesus are identified and concretized in Jesus crucified and raised. Therefore one may simply trust that the costly, vulnerable, serving, all-embracing and transforming love which comes to expression in Jesus flows forth from the heart of God. We can trust that this is true for the whole cosmos, all humanity and for ourselves. Two, I am convinced that the Abba and Spirit of Jesus are universally loose in the world and their presence and activity are within all creation and every people. We should never be surprised by the wondrous gift and consequences of that hope, that faith. Three, the heart and mind of the universe is one. "Hear O Israel, The Lord is one" (Deut 6) and the destiny of all reality and of all humanity is one in God who raised Jesus from the dead and poured out God's Spirit for the sake of all creation!

Acknowledgments

I wish to express my gratitude to The Reverend Rafael Malpica Padilla, the Director of ELCA Global Mission, for writing the Foreword.

This book is a revison of *The Word and the Way of the Cross*, published by the Division for Global Mission, The Evangelical Lutheran Church in America, 1993. Publication of this book is funded in part by a grant of ELCA Global Mission.

The revision deletes material which specifically related the first edition to "Commitments for Mission in the 1990's," a mission statement of the ELCA. It also includes a new first chapter that integrates the cross with Jesus' proclamation of the Kingdom of God. In my attempt to more clearly develop the central thesis of the book I have arranged the chapters and elements within the chapters in a different order. This makes it possible to outline my thoughts on Jesus, the Kingdom of God and the Cross before directly engaging in the critique of Christian witness found in 21st century Christian theology. It is hoped this will make the book more readable to those not acquainted with contemporary debates dealing with religious pluralism and clear up some mis-interpretations of my thesis.

Following my retirement from the Division for Global Mission in 1996, I became the Director of the Ph.D./Th.M Program for eight years at the Lutheran School of Theology at Chicago. During this period of time I was the Visiting Professor of Mission and taught courses dealing with Missiology, Interfaith Engagement and the Theology of the Cross. I often taught in teams with colleagues who have enriched my thought in the area of interfaith relationships. I wish to thank the Rev. Dirk Ficca, Director of the Parliament of World Religions for our classes dealing with religious pluralism and the mission of the church. His knowledge of the religious scene in Chicago was encyclopedic and his prophetic role within the Presbyterian Church made his sensitive theological position insightful.

I also profoundly thank Dr. G.H. Aasi, Professor of Islamic Studies at the American Islamic College in Chicago and Adjunt Professor at LSTC and Sensei Seven Ross, Director of the Chicago Zen Center who also is an Adjunct Professor at LSTC. Together we taught a number of courses. The conversations, dialogue and friendships outside and within our class sessions were deeply enriching and have influenced the tone and thought of this volume. Perhaps the gift of laughter, which so often filled the room, was a sign of future possibilities between our communities.

My profound gratitude also to the administration, faculty, students and staff of LSTC who welcomed me back into the academic world. Particular thanks are due to Dr. Ralph Klein who as Dean made my new assignment possible and to Dr. Harold Vogelaar, a colleague for many years, as we worked to engage the Evangelical Lutheran Church in America in Christian-Muslim dialogues.

Finally, I thank my daughter Sandra Lyons whose skills as a lawyer, research analyst and writer, made her an excellent editor of this manuscript.

Mark W. Thomsen

October, 2007

ACKNOWLEDGEMENTS—1993 Edition

This study in Christian mission and witness is the result of years of biblical and theological discussion with family, friends, students, missionaries and other colleagues. It would be impossible to recognize all of those who have contributed to the content of this volume; however, I do want to thank all of those who have voluntarily given hours of their time to work as members of a number of task forces which produced earlier mission documents which deeply influenced the present book.

The American Lutheran Church's Board for World Mission and Inter-Church Cooperation Task Force on Christian Witness

Among Muslims (1984-1986) produced *God and Jesus: Theological Reflections for Christian-Muslim Dialog,* 1986:

Dr. Willem A. Bijlefeld   Dr. Delvin D. Hutton
Dr. Carl E. Braaten   Dr. Robert W. Jenson
Dr. Terence E. Fretheim   Dr. Paul Varo Martenson

   The American Lutheran Church's Board for World Mission and Inter-Church Cooperation Task Force on Christian Witness Among Buddhists (1986-1988) produced *Suffering and Redemption: Exploring Christian Witness Within a Buddhist Context,* 1988:

Ms. Joyce Ditmanson   Dr. Paul Varo Martenson
Dr. Terence E. Fretheim   Dr. Merrill Morse
Dr. Theodore C. Fritchel   Dr. Paul R. Sponheim
Dr. Kosuke Koyama

   The Evangelical Lutheran Church in America's Task Force on a Mission Statement (1989-1990) produced *Commitments for Mission in the 1990's*:

Dr. Carl E. Braaten   Dr. William E. Lesher
Dr. Terence E. Fretheim   The Rev. Barbara Lundblad
Ms. Bonnie L. Jensen   Dr. Winston D. Persaud

   I also want to thank those who read the final drafts of *The Word and the Way of the Cross* and responded with critical suggestions: Dr. Willem A. Bijlefeld, Dr. James H. Burtness, The Rev. Michael G. Fonner, Dr. Terence E. Fretheim, Dr. Yoshiro Ishida, Ms. Bonnie L. Jensen, Dr. Paul Varo Martenson, Dr. Roland E. Miller, The Rev . Duane A. Olson, Dr. Edmund F. Perry, Dr. Duane A. Priebe and Dr. Paul R. Sponheim.

   I want to thank my wife, Mary Lou. For forty years we have shared a mission adventure. While in Africa in the 1950s and 1960s, she typed and edited earlier lectures and papers which became the foundation for *The Word and the Way of the Cross.* Finally, I wish to thank Ms. Karen Schneewind, who over the last ten years with meticulous skill has typed and edited innumerable drafts of all the mentioned documents.

Mark W. Thomsen, Executive Director
Division for Global Mission
Evangelical Lutheran Church in America
Chicago, Illinois, April 1993

Bibliography

Altman, Walter. "Interpreting the Doctrine of the Two Kingdoms." *Word and World*, Winter 1987.

Altman, Walter. *Luther and Liberation: A Latin American Perspective*. Minneapolis: Fortress Press, 1992.

The Amsterdam Declaration, 2000.

Ariarajah, Wesley. *The Bible and People of Other Faiths*. Geneva: World Council of Churches, 1985.

Ariarajah, Wesley. *Hindus and Christians: A Century of Protestant Ecumenical Thought*. Grand Rapids: Eerdmans Publishing, 1991.

Aulen, Gustav. *Christus Victor*. New York: Macmillan, 1931.

Baille, D.M. *God Was in Christ: An Essay on Incarnation and Atonement*. New York: Charles Scribner's Sons, 1955.

Barrett, David B. "Annual Statistical Table on Global Mission." *International Bulletin* 16 (January 1992):26.

Barth, Karl. *The Doctrine of the Word of God*. Vol. 1, part 1. *Prolegomena to Church Dogmatics*. Edinburgh: T. & T. Clark, 1936.

Berger, Peter. *The Sacred Canopy*. New York: Anchor Books, 1969.

Bijlefeld, Willem A. "Christian Witness in an Islamic Context," *God and Jesus: Theological Reflections for Christian Muslim Dialog* [1986]. Division of World Mission and Inter-Church Cooperation, The American Luther Church, Minneapolis, Minnesota. Photocopy. A collection of papers prepared by The American Luther Church's Board for World Mission and Inter-Church cooperation Task Force on Christian Witness Among Muslims, 1984-86.

Boer, Harry. *Pentecost and Missions*. London: Lutherworth, 1961.

Boff, Leonardo. *Way of the Cross–Way of Justice*. Maryknoll, NY: Orbis Books, 1982.

Boff, Leonardo and Boff, Clodovis. *Introducing Liberation Theology*. Maryknoll, NY: Orbis Books, 1987.

Bonhoeffer, Dietrich. *Letters and Papers from Prison*. London: Collins-S.C.M. Press, 1953; Enl. ed., New York: Macmillan Publishing, 1971.

Borg, Marcus J. *Jesus: A New Vision*. San Francisco: Harper & Row, 1987.

Braaten, Carl E. *The Apostolic Imperative*. Minneapolis: Augsburg Publishing, 1985.

Braaten, Carl E. *The Flaming Center: A Theology of Christian Mission World Religions*. Minneapolis: Fortress Press, 1992.

Braaten, Carl E. *No Other Gospel: Christianity Among the World Religions*. Minneapolis: Fortress Press, 1992.

Brimlow, Robert W. *What About Hitler? Wrestling with Jews*, Grand Rapids: Brazos Press, 2006.

Brunner, Emil. *The Word and the World*. London: S.C.M. Press, 1931.

Buddhadasa Bhikkhu. *Buddha-Dhamma for Students*. Translated by Ariyananda Bhikkhu (Roderick S. Bucknell). Rev. Ed. Chiang Mai, Thailand: Buddha-Nigama Association, 1972; reprint. Bangkok: Dhamma Study and Practice Group with help from Evolution/Liberation, 1988.

Butterfield, Herbert. *Christianity and History*. New York: Charles Scribner's Sons, 1949.

Castro, Emilio. *Freedom in Mission: The Perspective of the Kingdom of God*. Geneva: World Council of Churches, 1985.

Clendenin, Daniel B. *Many Gods, Many Lords: Christianity Encounters World Religions*. Grand Rapids, MI: Baker Books, 1995.

Cobb, John B., Jr. *Beyond Dialog: Toward a Mutual Transformation of Christianity and Buddhism*. Philadelphia: Fortress Press, 1982.

Cragg, Kenneth. *The Call of the Minaret*. Rev. ed. Maryknoll, NY: Orbis Books, 1989.

Cragg, Kenneth. *The Christ and the Faiths*. Philadelphia: Westminster Press, 1986.

Cragg, Kenneth. *Muhammad and the Christian: A Question of Response*. Maryknoll, NY: Orbis Books, 1984.

Crossan, John Dominic. *The Historical Jesus: The Life of a Mediterranean Jewish Peasant*. San Francisco: HarperCollins, 1991.

D'Costa, Gavin (ed). *Christian Uniqueness Reconsidered: The Myth of a Pluralistic Theology of Religions*. Maryknoll, NY: Orbis Books 1992.

Deane, S. N., trans. *Saint Anselm. Basic Writings: Proslogium, Monologium, and Appendix*. 1962. 2nd ed. Reprint. LaSalle, Illinois: Open Court Publishing, 1966.

Denny, Frederick Mathewson. *An Introduction to Islam*. New York: Macmillan Publishing, 1985.

Dominus Iusus VI, paragraph 22.

Dupuis, Jacques. *Toward a Christian Theology of Religious Pluralism*. Maryknoll, NY: Orbis Books, 1997.

Fiorenza, Elisabeth Schüssler. *In Memory of Her: A Feminist Theological Reconstruction of Christian Origins*. New York: Crossroad, 1984.

Forde, Gerhard. "Eleventh Locus, Christian Life, Justification Today." *Christian Dogmatics*. vol. 2. Edited by Carl Braaten and Robert Jenson. Philadelphia: Fortress Press, 1984.

Forell, George. *History of Christian Ethics*. vol. 1. Minneapolis: Augsburg Publishing, 1979.

Forell, George. *The Protestant Faith.* Englewood cliffs: Prentis-Hall, 1960.

Fretheim, Terence E. "God and Prophet: An Old Testament Perspective," *God and Jesus: Theological Reflections for Christian-Muslim Dialog.* [1986]. Division of World Mission and Inter-Church Cooperation, The American Lutheran Church, Minneapolis, Minnesota. Photocopy. A collection of papers prepared by the American Lutheran Church's board for World Mission and Inter-Church Cooperation Task Force on Christian Witness Among Muslims, 1984-1986.

Fretheim, Terence E. *The Suffering of God: An Old Testament Perspective.* Philadelphia: Fortress Press, 1984.

Gandi, M.K. *What Jesus Means to Me.* Compiled by R.K. Prabhu. Ahmedabad: Navajivan Publishing, 1959.

Gibb, H. A. R. *Mohammedanism: An Historical Survey.* 1949. 2nd ed. Reprinted with revisions. New York: Oxford University Press, 1962.

Gutierrez, Gustavo. *A Theology of Liberation: History, Politics and Salvation.* Maryknoll, NY: Orbis Books, 1973.

Hall, Douglas John. *God and Human Suffering: An Exercise in the Theology of the Cross.* Minneapolis: Augsburg Publishing, 1986.

Hauerwas, Stanley and Willimon, William H. *Resident Aliens.* Nashville: Abingdon, 1989.

Heim, S. Mark. *Salvation: Truth and Difference in Religion.* Maryknoll, NY: Orbis Books, 1995.

Hick, John. "Whatever Path Men Choose is Mine." *Christianity and Other Religions: Selected Readings.* Edited by John Hick and Brian Hebblethwaithe. Philadelphia: Fortress Press, 1981.

Hick, John and Knitter, Paul F. *The Myth of Christian Uniqueness.* Maryknoll, NY: Orbis Books, 1987.

Jenson, Robert W. *The Triune Identity.* Philadelphia: Fortress Press, 1982.

"Justification and Justice." *Word and World*, Winter 1987: 3-98.

Kierkegaard, Søren. *Training in Christianity.* Translated with introductory notes by Walter Lowrie. London: Oxford University Press, 1941.

Kitamori, Kazo. *The Theology of the Pain of God.* Richmond: John Knox Press, 1965.

Knitter, Paul F. *Jesus and the Other Names: Christian Mission and Global Responsibility.* Maryknoll, NY: Orbis Books 1996.

Knitter, Paul F. *No Other Name? A Critical Survey of Christian Attitudes Toward the World Religions.* Maryknoll, NY: Orbis Books, 1985.

Knitter, Paul F. *One Earth Many Religions.* Maryknoll, NY: Orbis Books, 1995.

Koyama, Kosuke. *Waterbuffalo Theology.* Maryknoll, NY: Orbis Books, 1974.

Küng, Hans. "The World Religions in God's Plan of Salvation" in *Christian Revelation and World Religions,* ed. Joseph Neuner. London: Burns and Oates, 1967.

Luther, Martin. *Martin Luther's Basic Theological Writings.* Edited by Timothy F. Lull. Minneapolis: Fortress Press, 1989.

Martinson, Paul Varo. *A Theology of World Religions.* Minneapolis: Augsburg Publishing 1987.

Martinson, Paul Varo. "Do Our Pathways Cross?" *Suffering and Redemption: Exploring Christian Witness Within a Buddhist Context* [1988]. Division of Global Mission, Evangelical Lutheran Church in American, Chicago, Illinois. Photocopy. A collection of papers prepared by The American Lutheran Church's Board for World Mission and Inter-Church Cooperation Task Force on Christian Witness Among Buddhists, 1986-1988.

Mollenkott, Virginia Ramey. *The Divine Feminine: The Biblical Imagery of God as Female.* New York: Crossroad, 1989.

Moltmann, Jürgen. *The Crucified God: The Cross of Christ as the Foundation and Criticism of Christian Theology.* New York: Harper & Row, 1974.

NCC Statement *Interfaith Relations and the Churches,* section "Jesus Christ and Reconciliation.

Newbigin, Lesslie. *Trinitarian Faith and Today's Mission.* Richmond: John Knox Press, 1963.

Niebuhr, Reinhold. *The Nature and Destiny of Man: A Christian Interpretation.* Vol. 1. New York: Charles Schribner's Sons, 1955.

Nygren, Anders. *The Essence of Christianity.* Philadelphia: Muhlenberg Press, 1961.

Pannenberg, Wolfhart. *Jesus–God and Man.* Translated by Lewis L. Wilkens and Duane A. Priebe. Philadelphia: Westminister Press, 1968.

Pannenberg, Wolfhart. "The Religions from the Perspective of Christian Theology and the Self-Interpretation of Christianity in Relation to Non-Christian Religions," *Modern Theology* 9:3, July 1993.

Pannenberg, Wolfhart. "Toward a Theology of the History of Religions," *Basic Questions in Theology,* vol. 2. Philadelphia: Fortress Press, 1971.

Rahbar, Daud. *God of Justice: A Study in Ethical Doctrine of the Qur'an.* Leiden, the Netherlands: E.J. Brill 1960.

Rahbar, Daud. "Memories and Meanings" [1985]. Boston University. Photocopy.

Rahman, Fazlur. *Major Themes of the Qur'an.* Minneapolis: Bibliotheca Islamica, 1989.

Rahner, Karl. "Christianity and the Non-Christian Religions" in *Christianity and Other Religions,* eds. John Hick and Brian Hebbelthwaite. Philadelphia: Fortress Press, 1981.

Rahner, Karl. *Theological Investigations,* vol. 5.

Rahula, Walpola Sri. *What the Buddha Taught.* New York: Grove Press, 1974.

Redemptoris Missio, paragraph 55, "Dialogue With our Brothers and Sisters of Other Religions" 1990.

Saint Anselm. Basic Writings, Proslogium, Monologium, and Appendix. Translated by S.N. Deane. 2nd ed. 1962. Reprint. LaSalle, Illinois: Open Court Publishing, 1966.

Song, Choan-Seng. *Third Eye Theology: Theology in Formation in Asian Settings.* Rev. ed. Maryknoll, NY: Orbis Books, 1979.

Sponheim, Paul. "To Know God in Experience" *Suffering and Redemption: Exploring Christian Witness Within a Buddhist Context*, 1988.

Suzuki, Daisetz Teitaro. *An Introduction to Zen Buddhism*. New York: Grove Press, 1964.

Swidler, Leonard and Mojzes, Paul (eds). *The Uniqueness of Jesus: A Dialogue with Paul Knitter.* Maryknoll, NY: Orbis Books, 1997.

Tappert, Theodore G. trans. and ed. *The Book of Concord: The Confessions of the Evangelical Lutheran Church.* Philadelphia: Fortress Press, 1959.

Thomsen, Mark. "A Christology of the Spirit." *Dialog* 16 (Spring 1977): 135-138.

Thomsen, Mark. *Christ Crucified: A 21st Century Missiology of the Cross.* Minneapolis: Lutheran University Press, 2004.

Thomsen, Mark. "Into Arabia." *Currents in Theology and Mission,* June 2006.

Thomsen, Mark. "The Lordship of Jesus and Theological Pluralism." *Dialog* 9 (1972): 125ff.

Thomsen, Mark. *The Word and the Way of the Cross: Christian Witness Among Muslim and Buddhist People.* Chicago: The Evangelical Lutheran Church in America, Division of Global Mission, 1993.

Tillich, Paul. "Existence and the Christ." *Systematic Theology.* Vol. 2. Chicago: University of Chicago Press, 1957.

Tillich, Paul. Systematic Theology. Vol. 3. Chicago: University of Chicago Press, 1963.

Tutu, Desmond. "The Theology of Liberation in Africa." *African Theology en Route, Papers from the Pan-African Conference of Third World Theologians, December 17-23, 1977, Accra, Ghana.* Edited by Kofi Appiah-Kubi and Sergio Torres. Maryknoll, NY: Orbis Books, 1979.

von Loewenich, Walther. *Luther's Theology of the Cross.* Minneapolis: Augsburg Publishing House, 1961.

Watt, W. Montgomery. *Muhammed: Prophet and Statesman.* Oxford: Oxford University Press, 1961.

World Christian Encyclopedia, Vol.1. 2nd ed. Edited by David B. Barrett, George T. Kurian and Tod M. Johnson. Oxford University Press.

Yoder, John H. *The Politics of Jesus: Vicit Agnus Noster.* Grand Rapids: Eerdmans Publishing, 1972.

Endnotes

Introduction

[1] World Christian Encyclopedia, Vol.1,2nd edition, eds. David B. Barrett, George T. Kurian and Tod M. Johnson (Oxford University Press).

[2] John Kasserow in a Ph.D. dissertation has presented striking documentation of an earlier contact with 3rd and 4th century Alexandrian Christianity. (A copy is available at the Catholic Theological Union Library in Chicago.)

Chapter 1: The Presence of the Kingdom of God

[3] Choan-Seng Song, *Third Eye Theology: Theology in Formation in Asian Settings* (Maryknoll, New York: Orbis Books, 1979, revised edition), 181 (hereafter cited as *Third Eye Theology*).

[4] Carl Braaten, *The Apostolic Imperative* (Minneapolis: Augsburg Publishing House, 1985).

[5] Harry Boer, *Pentecost and Missions* (London: Lutherworth, 1961).

[6] Lesslie Newbigin, *Trinitarian Faith and Today's Mission* (Richmond: John Knox Press, 1963).

[7] Emilio Castro, *Freedom in Mission: The Perspective of the Kingdom of God* (Geneva: World Council of Churches, 1985).

[8] Song, *Third Eye Theology*, 108.

Chapter 2: God's Radical Mission Identified

[9] Gustav Aulen, *Christus Victor* (New York: Macmillan, 1931).

[10] Large Catechism and Small Catechism in *The Book of Concord*, (Minneapolis: Fortress Press, 1959) the Second Article of the Creed and its meaning (see both), 345,413-415.

[11] Copyright©1978 *Lutheran Book of Worship*. Reprinted by permission of Augsburg Fortress.

[12] Walter Altmann, *Luther and Liberation: A Latin American Perspective* (Minneapolis: Fortress Press, 1992).

[13] Altmann, *Luther and Liberation: A Latin American Perspective*, 24.

[14] Altmann, *Luther and Liberation: A Latin American Perspective*, 25.

[15] Gustavo Gutierrez, *A Theology of Liberation: History, Politics and Salvation* (Maryknoll, New York: Orbis Books, 1973), 228-232. See also Song, *Third Eye Theology*, 218ff.

[16] Leonardo Boff, *Way of the Cross—Way of Justice* (Maryknoll, New York: Orbis Books, 1982), 89. Boff wrote this fascinating book, at the end of seven years of christological study and six major publications dealing with Christology.

[17] Boff, *Way of the Cross—Way of Justice*, ix.

[18] Marcus J. Borg, *Jesus: A New Vision* (San Francisco: Harper & Row, 1987), 184.

[19] The theological focus upon liberation within the context of poverty and oppression has literally encircled the globe: Black theology in Africa, Minjung theology in Korea, and Dalit theology in India. The theme has permeated almost every theological movement and confessional family in the world.

[20] The picture of Jesus being on the other side of the line comes from lectures and conversations with Dr. Duane Priebe of Wartburg Theological Seminary, Dubuque, Iowa.

[21] Borg, *Jesus: A New Vision*, 86.

[22] Borg, *Jesus: A New Vision*, 89.

[23] Borg, *Jesus: A New Vision*, 131-141.

[24] Borg, *Jesus: A New Vision*, 82.

[25] Leonardo and Clodovis Boff, *Introducing Liberation Theology* (Maryknoll, New York: Orbis Books, 1987), chaps. 2 and 3.

[26] Desmond Tutu, "The Theology of Liberation in Africa," in *African Theology en Route, Papers from the Pan-African Conference of Third World Theologians, December 17-23, 1977, Accra, Ghana*, Kofi Appiah-Kubi and Sergio Torres, eds. (Maryknoll, New York: Orbis Books, 1979), 168.

[27] John Dominic Crossan, *The Historical Jesus: The Life of a Mediterranean Jewish Peasant* (San Francisco: HarperCollins, 1991). See chaps. 9 and 10.

[28] John H. Yoder, *The Politics of Jesus: Vicit Agnus Noster* (Grand Rapids: Eerdmans Publishing, 1972), 32.

[29] Timothy F. Lull, ed., *Martin Luther's Basic Theological Writings* (Minneapolis: Fortress Press, 1989), 30.

[30] Dietrich Bonhoeffer, *Letters and Papers from Prison* (London: Collins-S.C.M. Press, 1953), 122, (New York: Macmillan Publishing, 1971, new enlarged ed.), 360-361.

[31] Kazo Kitamori, *The Theology of the Pain of God* (Richmond: John Knox Press, 1965 ed.), 119-121. For a recent and exceptional study of the suffering of God in the Old Testament, see Terence E. Fretheim's book *The Suffering of God: An Old Testament Perspective* (Philadelphia: Fortress Press, 1984), Chap. 7 for a discussion similar to Kitamori's. Fretheim has two contributions in "God and Jesus: Theological Reflections for Christian-Muslim Dialog" (Division for World Mission and Inter-Church Cooperation, The American Lutheran Church, 1986, Photocopied) which articulate his unique contribution to theology in this area of biblical study.

[32] Robert W. Jenson, *The Triune Identity* (Philadelphia: Fortress Press, 1982), 39.

[33] See Kenneth Cragg, *The Call of the Minaret*, revised (Maryknoll, New York: Orbis, 1989), 272.

[34] Jürgen Moltmann, *The Crucified God: The Cross of Christ as the Foundation and Criticism of Christian Theology* (New York: Harper and Row, 1974), 235-249 (hereafter cited as *The Crucified God*). For another interpretation of the atonement grounded in the unity of God and Jesus, see *The Essence of Christian-*

ity by Anders Nygren (Philadelphia: Muhlenberg Press, 1961), 126-128. Nygren grounds atonement in God's willingness to pour out costly love upon selfish humanity even though it is spurned and trampled upon. This love designated "lost love" is the atonement.

[35] Moltmann, *The Crucified God*, 243.

[36] Moltmann, *The Crucified God*, 245.

[37] Moltmann, *The Crucified God*, 248.

[38] Douglas John Hall, *God and Human Suffering: An Exercise in the Theology of the Cross* (Minneapolis: Augsburg Publishing House, 1986), 113 (hereafter cited as *God and Human Suffering*).

[39] Hall, *God and Human Suffering*, 98.

[40] Hall, *God and Human Suffering*, 109.

[41] Fretheim, The Suffering of God: An Old Testament Perspective (Philadelphia: Fortress Press, 1984) (hereafter cited as *The Suffering of God*).

[42] Fretheim, *The Suffering of God*, 127.

[43] Fretheim, *The Suffering of God*, 128.

[44] Fretheim, *The Suffering of God*, 128.

[45] Fretheim, *The Suffering of God*; see chaps. 8 and 9 for an excellent discussion of this topic.

[46] Koyama, *Waterbuffalo Theology*, chaps. 9, 11 and 13.

[47] Song, *Third Eye Theology*, 184, cf Rom 8:38-39.

[48] The following three paragraphs are from a letter written August 27, 1990, to an ELCA missionary and copied to several others who challenged this double affirmation of the suffering of God.

[49] D. M. Baillie, *God Was In Christ: An Essay on Incarnation and Atonement* (New York: Charles Scribner's Sons, 1955), 194.

[50] Kenneth Cragg, *Muhammad and the Christian: A Question of Response* (Maryknoll, New York: Orbis, 1984), 138.

Chapter 3: Contemporary Challenges

[51] Wesley Ariarajah, *Hindus and Christians: A Century of Protestant Ecumenical Thought* (Grand Rapids: Eerdmans Publishing, 1991) (hereafter cited as *Hindus and Christians*).

[52] Kosuke Koyama, *Waterbuffalo Theology* (Maryknoll, New York: Orbis, 1974), 209ff.

[53] Ariarajah, *Hindus and Christians*, 211.

[54] Wesley Ariarajah, *The Bible and People of Other Faiths* (Geneva: World Council of Churches, 1985), xiv.

[55] Ariarajah, *The Bible and People of Other Faiths*, 2.

[56] Ariarajah, *The Bible and People of Other Faiths.* 3.

[57] Ariarajah, *The Bible and People of Other Faiths*, 5ff.

[58] Ariarajah, *The Bible and People of Other Faiths*, 7.

[59] Ariarajah, *The Bible and People of Other Faiths*, 11.

[60] Ariarajah, *The Bible and People of Other Faiths*, 21.

[61] Ariarajah, *The Bible and People of Other Faiths*, 13-18.

[62] Ariarajah, *The Bible and People of Other Faiths*, 13.

[63] For excellent surveys of these views, see Paul Knitter's *No Other Name?* and Wesley Ariarajah's *Hindus and Christians*.

[64] Carl Braaten, *No Other Gospel: Christianity Among the World's Religions* (Minneapolis: Fortress Press, 1992), 3 (hereafter cited as *No Other Gospel*).

[65] Braaten, *No Other Gospel*, 10.

[66] Braaten, *No Other Gospel*, 11; see also Braaten's *The Flaming Center: A Theology of Christian Mission* (Philadelphia: Fortress Press, 1977), 93-119 (hereafter cited as *The Flaming Center*).

[67] Braaten, *No Other Gospel*.

[68] Braaten, *No Other Gospel*, 2.

[69] Braaten, *No Other Gospel*, 47.

[70] Braaten, *No Other Gospel*, 11.

[71] Braaten, *No Other Gospel*, 38.

[72] John Hick, "Whatever Path Men Choose is Mine," in *Christianity and Other Religions: Selected Readings,* eds. John Hick and Brian Hebblethwaite (Philadelphia: Fortress Press, 1981), 177-78.

[73] Hick, "Whatever Path Men Choose is Mine," 186.

[74] Hick, "Whatever Path Men Choose is Mine," 186.

[75] Paul F. Knitter, *No Other Name: A Critical Survey of Christian Attitude Toward the World Religions* (Maryknoll, New York: Orbis, 1985), 231 (hereafter cited as *No Other Name*). **For the later development of Knitter's "normative" discussion and the contemporary pluralism debate see Appendix II.** (from my *Christ Crucified: A 21ˢᵗ Century Missiology of the Cross* (Minneapolis: Lutheran University Press, Chapter 3).

[76] Carl Braaten, *The Apostolic Imperative* (Minneapolis: Augsburg Publishing House, 1985), 14.

[77] Knitter, *No Other Name*, 182.

[78] Ariarajah, *The Bible and People of Other Faiths*, 25.

[79] Knitter, *No Other Name*, 185.

[80] Knitter, *No Other Name*, 182.

[81] Ariarajah, *The Bible and People of Other Faiths*, 26.

[82] Ariarajah, *The Bible and People of Other Faiths*, 31.

[83] Ariarajah, *The Bible and People of Other Faiths*, 32.

[84] Ariarajah, *The Bible and People of Other Faiths*, 32.

[85] Ariarajah, *The Bible and People of Other Faiths*, 70-71.

[86] Koyama, *Waterbuffalo Theology*, 209ff.

[87] Carl Braaten has a chap. in *The Apostolic Imperative* entitled "The Cross as the Criterion of Christianity," 16-32.

Chapter 4: Jesus' Call to Discipleship

[88] Altmann, *Luther and Liberation: A Latin American Perspective*, 24-25.

[89] Yoder, *The Politics of Jesus*, 115ff.

[90] Altmann, *Luther and Liberation: A Latin American Perspective*, 24-25.

[91] For a discussion relating to this concern in contemporary Lutheran circles, see the 1987 Winter issue of *Word and World* entitled "Justification and Justice." Twenty-nine theologians from all of the Americas debated concerning the relationship between the gospel and discipleship committed to justice.

[92] Small Catechism in *The Book of Concord*, (Philadelphia: Fortress Press, 1959) 349.

[93] Lull, *Martin Luther's Basic Theological Writings*, 597.

[94] Lull, *Martin Luther's Basic Theological Writings*, 610.

[95] Lull, *Martin Luther's Basic Theological Writings*, 611.

[96] Lull, *Martin Luther's Basic Theological Writings*, 612.

[97]Lull, *Martin Luther's Basic Theological Writings*, 618.

[98]Lull, *Martin Luther's Basic Theological Writings*, 619-620.

[99]Gerhard Forde, "Eleventh Locus, Christian Life, Justification Today," in *Christian Dogmatics*, vol. 2, ed. by Carl Braaten and Robert Jenson (Philadelphia: Fortress Press, 1984), 468.

[100]Bonhoeffer, *Letters and Papers from Prison*, 1953 ed., 123.

[101]Altman, *Luther and Liberation: A Latin American Perspective*, 24-25.

[102]Stanley Hauerwas and William H. Willimon in *Resident Aliens* (Nashville: Abingdon, 1989), develop a Christian ethic around the theme that Christians live as aliens in contemporary culture.

[103]Søren Kierkegaard, *Training in Christianity*, translated with introductory notes by Walter Lowrie (London: Oxford University Press, 1941), 40, 58, 173.

[104]Elisabeth Schüssler Fiorenza, *In Memory of Her: A Feminist Theological Reconstruction of Christian Origins* (New York: Crossroad, 1984), 34.

[105]Virginia Ramey Mollenkott, *The Divine Feminine: The Biblical Imagery of God as Female* (New York: Crossroad, 1989).

[106]Braaten, *The Apostolic Imperative*, 75.

[107]For a discussion of mission as rooted in the presence of God's future in Christ, see: Carl Braaten's, *The Flaming Center*, chap. 2, 39-63.

[108]Ariarajah, *The Bible and People of Other Faiths*, 70.

[109]Yoder, *The Politics of Jesus*, 250.

[110]George Forell, *History of Christian Ethics*, vol 1 (Minneapolis: Augsburg Publishing, 1979), 58.

[111]Forell, *History of Christian Ethics*, vol 1, 60.

[112]Lull, *Martin Luther's Basic Theological Writings, Temporal Authority*, 668.

[113]Lull, *Martin Luther's Basic Theological Writings*, 668.

[114]Lull, *Martin Luther's Basic Theological Writings*, 669.

[115]Lull, *Martin Luther's Basic Theological Works*, 670.

[116]Braaten, *The Flaming Center*, 58.

[117]Braaten, *The Flaming Center*, 58-62.

[118]Walter Altmann, "Interpreting the Doctrine of the Two Kingdoms," *Word and World*, Winter 1987, 54-55.

[119]Altmann, "Interpreting the Doctrine of the Two Kingdoms," 55.

[120]Putting Luther's two kingdom thought into biblical kingdom of God terms; that is, "the present age" and "the new or coming age" can be of assistance. I thank Graydon Snyder of Chicago Theological Seminary for discussions which have been of assistance in this area.

[121]Brimlow, Robert W., *What about Hitler?: Wrestling with Jews*, Grand Rapids. MI.: Brazos Press, 2006.

Chapter 5: Dialogue and Witness

[122]Fazlur Rahman, *Major Themes of the Qur'an* (Minneapolis: Bibliotheca Islamica, 1989), 144.

[123]John B. Cobb, Jr., *Beyond Dialog: Toward a Mutual Transformation of Christianity and Buddhism* (Philadelphia: Fortress Press, 1982).

[124]M. K. Gandhi, *What Jesus Means to Me*, compiled by R. K. Prabhu (Ahmedabad: Navajivan Publishing, 1959), 4.

Chapter 6: Engaging with Muslim Peoples

[125] Daud Rahbar, *God of Justice: A Study in Ethical Doctrine of the Qur'an* (Leiden, The Netherlands: E. J. Brill, 1960).

[126] Rahbar, *God of Justice*, xii.

[127] Rahman, *Major Themes of the Qur'an*, 29.

[128] Daud Rahbar, "Memories and Meanings" (Boston University, 1985, Photocopied), 359-360.

[129] Rahman, *Major Themes of the Qur'an*, 9.

[130] It is interesting to note that it is exactly in Christ's weakness and suffering that Dietrich Bonhoeffer sees the possibility of humanity coming of age and taking responsibility for life in the world: "This is the decisive difference between Christianity and all religions. Man's religiosity makes him look in his distress to the power of God in the world; he uses God as a *Deus ex machina* [literally 'God out of a machine' from ancient dramas where Gods were let down from above to save someone in distress]. The Bible, however, directs him to the powerlessness and suffering of God; only a suffering God can help." A suffering God calls humanity to come of age taking responsibility for life. (From *Letters and Papers from Prison*, 122, 174.)

[131] Rahman, *Major Themes of the Qur'an*, 30.

[132] Rahman, *Major Themes of the Qur'an*, 30.

[133] Rahman, *Major Themes of the Qur'an*, 29-30.

[134] Rahbar, *Memories and Meanings*, 350.

[135] Kenneth Cragg, *The Christ and the Faiths* (Philadelphia: Westminster Press, 1986), 324.

[136] Surah 4:171, also 5:117; 5:72-75.

[137] Rahman, *Major Themes of the Qur'an*, 168.

[138] Rahman, *Major Themes of the Qur'an*, 170.

[139] Rahman, *Major Themes of the Qur'an*, 13.

[140] Jenson, *The Triune Identity*, 33.

[141] Terence Fretheim, "God and Prophet: An Old Testament Perspective," *God and Jesus: Theological Reflections for Christian-Muslim Dialog* (Collection of papers prepared by The American Lutheran Church's Board for World Mission and Inter-Church Cooperation Task Force on Christian Witness Among Muslims, Minneapolis, Minnesota, 1984-86, Photocopied), 38. See also Appendix 1 of the first edition of this volume.

[142] Fretheim, *God and Jesus: Theological Reflections for Christian-Muslim Dialog*, 42.

[143] Kenneth Cragg, *The Call of the Minaret*, rev. ed. (Maryknoll, New York: Orbis, 1989), 244.

[144] Willem A. Bijlefeld, "Christian Witness in an Islamic Context," *God and Jesus: Theological Reflections for Christian Muslim Dialog*, 77. See note 146.

[145] Cragg, *Call of the Minaret*, 263.

[146] Rahman, *Major Themes of the Qur'an*, 170.

[147] For some Muslims this would not be a significant point. Dr. Willem Bijlefeld quotes Dr. Isma'il Al-Faruqi who once said, "God does not reveal himself. He does not reveal himself to anyone in anyway. God reveals only His will." (From "God and Jesus: Theological Reflections for Christian-Muslim Dialog," 73.)

[148] Frederick Mathewson Denny, *An Introduction to Islam* (New York: Macmillan Publishing, 1985), 201-202.

[149] This particular Trinitarian terminology is derived from Karl Barth, *Church Dogmatics: The Doctrine of the Word of God*, vol. 1 (Edinburgh: T. & T. Clark, 1936), 417.

[150] Rahman, *Major Themes of the Qur'an*, 170.

[151] Rahman, *Major Themes of the Qur'an*, 86.

[152] Rahman, *Major Themes of the Qur'an*, 87.

[153] Cragg, *The Call of the Minaret*, 268.

[154] Cragg, *The Call of the Minaret*, 268.

[155] Cragg, *The Call of the Minaret*, 268.

[156] W. Montgomery Watt entitles his book on Muhammad, *Muhammad: Prophet and Statesman* (Oxford: Oxford University Press, 1961).

[157] Rahman, *Major Themes of the Qur'an*, 62.

[158] H. A. R. Gibb, *Mohammedanism: An Historical Survey*, 2nd ed. (1949; Reprint, New York: Oxford University Press, 1962), 90.

[159] Rahman, *Major Themes of the Qur'an*, 53.

[160] Rahman, *Major Themes of the Qur'an*, 64.

[161] Rahman, *Major Themes of the Qur'an*, 63-64.

[162] Rahman, *Major Themes of the Qur'an*, 63.

Chapter 7: Engaging With Buddhist Peoples

[163] Walpola Sri Rahula, *What the Buddha Taught* (New York: Grove Press, 1974), 1.

[164] Paul Martinson, "Do Our Pathways Cross?" *Suffering and Redemption: Exploring Christian Witness Within a Buddhist Context* (Collection of papers prepared by The American Lutheran Church's Board for World Mission and Inter-Church Cooperation Task Force on Christian Witness Among Buddhists, Minneapolis, Minnesota, 1986-88, Photocopied), 93 (hereafter cited as *Suffering and Redemption*).

[165] Daisetz Teitaro Suzuki, *An Introduction to Zen Buddhism* (New York: Grove Press, 1964), 44.

[166] Rahula, *What the Buddha Taught*, 52.

[167] Rahula, *What the Buddha Taught*, 20ff.

[168] Rahula, *What the Buddha Taught*, 13.

[169] Paul Sponheim, "To Know God in Experience," *Suffering and Redemption*, 106ff.

[170] See Appendix 1 of the first edition of this book.

[171] See Wolfhart Pannenberg, *Jesus–God and Man*, trans. by Lewis L. Wilkens and Duane A. Priebe (Philadelphia: Westminister Press, 1968), chap. 3, particularly page 131. For a critical affirmation of Pannenberg's thesis see Mark Thomsen, "The Lordship of Jesus and Theological Pluralism," *Dialog*, vol. 9, 1972, 125ff.

[172] Rahula, *What the Buddha Taught*, 16ff, for a description of *dukkha*.

[173] George Forell, *The Protestant Faith* (Englewood Cliffs: Prentis-Hall, 1960), 133ff; Paul Tillich, "Existence and the Christ," *Systematic Theology* (Chicago: University of Chicago Press, 1957), vol. 2, 44ff.

[174] Reinhold Niebuhr, *The Nature and Destiny of Man: A Christian Interpretation*, vol. 1 (New York: Charles Scribner's Sons, 1955), chap. 7, 186ff.

[175] Rahula, *What the Buddha Taught*, 50ff.

[176] Rahula, *What the Buddha Taught*, 29.

[177] Rahula, *What the Buddha Taught*, 35.

[178] Buddhadasa Bhikkhu, *Buddha-Dhamma for Students, rev. ed.* (Bangkok: Dhamma Study and Practice Group, revised 1988), 52-53.

[179] Buddhadasa, *Buddha-Dhamma for Students*, 39.

[180] Rahula, *What the Buddha Taught*, 43.

[181] Cor 15:20 where Jesus is "the first fruits of those who have died."
[182] Rahula, *What the Buddha Taught*, 46.
[183] Rahula, *What the Buddha Taught*, 86.
[184] Rahula, *What the Buddha Taught*, 84.
[185] Rahula, *What the Buddha Taught*, 68.

Chapter 8: A Call to Radical Witness

[186] Mark Thomsen, "Withdrawal for Reflection", *Currents in Theology and Mission*, June 2006,253.
[187] Herbert Butterfield, *Christianity and History* (New York: Charles Scribner's Sons, 1949), 146.
[188] Paul Tillich, *Systematic Theology*, vol. 3 (Chicago: University of Chicago Press, 1963), 155.
[189] Emil Brunner, *The Word and the World* (London: S.C.M. Press, 1931), 108.
[190] For a recent discussion of this topic, see chapter 5 in Paul Varo Martinson's *A Theology of World Religions* (Minneapolis: Augsburg Publishing, 1987), 215ff.
[191] Herbert Butterfield, *Christianity and History* (New York: Charles Scribner's Sons, 1949), 146.

Appendix I: A Theological Proposal

[192] *God and Jesus: Theological Reflections for Christian-Muslim Dialog.* See note 146.
[193] *God and Jesus: Theological Reflections for Christian-Muslim Dialog*, 57.
[194] *God and Jesus: Theological Reflections for Christian-Muslim Dialog*, 63.
[195] *God and Jesus: Theological Reflections for Christian-Muslim Dialog*, 62.
[196] *God and Jesus: Theological Reflections for Christian-Muslim Dialog*, 5.
[197] I have made a similar argument for "A Christology of the Spirit" in *Dialog*, 16 (Spring 1977), 135-138.

Appendix II: Religious Pluralism

[198] Peter Benger, *The Sacred Canopy* (New York: Anchor Books, 1969), Chap. 1.
[199] The Amsterdam Declaration, no. 6.
[200] Ibid. no. 5.
[201] Rahner, "Christianity and the Non-Christian Religions" in *Christianity and Other Religions,* ed. John Hick and Brian Hebbelthwaite (Philadelphia: Fortress Press, 1981), p. 63. See also Karl Rahner, *Theological Investigations,* vol. 5.
[202] Ibid. p. 75.
[203] Hans Kung, "The World Religions in God's Plan of Salvation" in *Christian Revelation and World Religions,* ed. Joseph Neuner (London: Burns and Oates, 1967), p. 51ff.
[204] *Redemptoris Missio,* paragraph 55, "Dialogue With Our Brothers and Sisters of Other Religions," 1990.
[205] Dominus Iesus VI, paragraph 22.
[206] Genesis 14.18-20.
[207] Proverbs 8.15-16.
[208] Rom 2.14-16.
[209] Kurt Hendel, professor of historical theology at the Lutheran School of Theology in Chicago makes this statement.
[210] Wolfhart Pannenberg, "The Religions from the Perspective of Christian Theology and the Self-Interpretation of Christianity in Relation to Non-Christian Religions," *Modern Theology* 9:3, July 1993, pp. 285-297.

211 See e.g. Wolfhart Pannenberg, "Toward a Theology of the History of Religions," *Basic Questions in Theology,* vol. II (Philadelphia: Fortress Press, 1971), pp. 65-118; Carl E. Braaten, "The Gospel of Salvation and the World Religions," chap. 4 of *The Flaming Center: A Theology of Christian Mission* (Philadelphia: Fortress Press, 1977), pp. 93-119; Carl E. Braaten *No Other Gospel: Christianity Among the World Religions* (Minneapolis: Fortress Press, 1992), pp. 65-81.

212 NCC Statement *Interfaith Relations and the Churches,* section "Jesus Christ and Reconciliation."

213 Paul F. Knitter, No Other Name? A Critical Survey of Christian Attitudes Toward the World Religions (Maryknoll, NY: Orbis Books, 1985).

214 John Hick and Paul Knitter, Ed. *The Myth of Christian Uniqueness* (Maryknoll, NY: Orbis Books, 1987).

215 Ibid. p. viii.

216 Daniel B. Clendenin, *Many Gods, Many Lords: Christianity Encounters World Religions* (Grand Rapids, MI: Baker Books, 1995), p. 31.

217 Gordon D. Kaufmann, op. cit. p. 9.

218 Knitter op. cit. p. x.

219 Knitter op. cit. p. xi.

220 Rosemary Ruetter, op. cit. p. 141.

221 Christian Uniqueness Reconsidered: The Myth of a Pluralistic Theology of Religions, ed. Gavin D'Costa (Maryknoll, NY: Orbis Books), p. xxii.

222 Ibid., John Cobb, pp. 81ff; J.A. DiNoia, pp. 119ff.

223 Ibid., DiNoia, pp. 119-134; Surin, pp. 192 ff.

224 Ibid., M.M. Thomas, pp. 49ff.

225 Mark Thomsen, *The Word and the Way of the Cross: Christian Witness Among Muslim and Buddhist People* (Chicago: The Evangelical Lutheran Church in America, Division for Global Mission, 1993).

226 Gilkey, op. cit. ed. Hick and Knitter, pp. 44-45.

227 *The Uniqueness of Jesus: A Dialogue with Paul Knitter,* ed. Leonard Swidler and Paul Mojzes (Maryknoll, NY: Orbis Books, 1997); Paul F. Knitter, *Jesus and the Other Names* (Maryknoll, NY: Orbis Books, 1996); Paul F. Knitter, *One Earth Many Religions* (Maryknoll, NY: Orbis Books, 1995).

228 Paul Knitter, *One Earth Many Religions* (Maryknoll, NY: Orbis Books, 1995), p. 181.

229 Paul Knitter, *Jesus and the Other Names* (Maryknoll, NY: Orbis Books, 1996), note pp. 10-11, where Knitter describes his life experiences that moved him to take justice issues seriously.

230 Ibid. pp. 17-19.

231 Ibid. p. 19.

232 Ibid. p. 23.

233 *The Uniqueness of Jesus: A Dialogue with Paul Knitter,* ed. Leonard Swidler and Paul Mojzes (Maryknoll, NY: Orbis Books, 1997), pp. 152-154.

234 Paul Knitter, *Jesus and the Other Names: Christian Mission and Global Responsibility* (Maryknoll, NY: Orbis Books, 1996), pp. 73-83; and *The Uniqueness of Jesus: A Dialogue with Paul Knitter,* ed. Leonard Swidler and Paul Mojzes (Maryknoll, NY: Orbis Books,1997), pp. 7-11, 155-161.

235 Jesus and the Other Names, 79.

236 *The Uniqueness of* Jesus, 182. It probably should be noted that the pluralists John Hick and Raimon Panniker think that Knitter has conceded too much to his critics. See Hick pp. 79ff and Panniker pp. 111ff.

[237] The Uniqueness of Jesus, 155.

[238] See *The Uniqueness of Jesus, n.* 20 on 14-15 and 155 ff.

[239] See The Uniqueness of Jesus, n. 5 on 157 and 158.

[240] The Uniqueness of Jesus, 11.

[241] Ibid., 13.

[242] Heim, 101-110.

[243] Heim, 214.

[244] Heim, 224.

[245] Heim, 124.

[246] Heim, 133-136.

[247] Heim, 145.

[248] Heim, 215.

[249] Heim, 149.

[250] Heim, 177.

[251] Heim, 160.

[252] Heim, 167.

[253] Heim, 217.

[254] Heim, 215.

[255] For an evaluation of Heim from a Catholic perspective see *Toward a Christian Theology of Religious Pluralism* by Jacques Dupuis (Maryknoll, NY: Orbis Books, 1997).